# An Introduction to Good Saving Habits

*Discover Simple Methods to Change Your Financial Situation*

# An Introduction to Good Saving Habits

*Discover Simple Methods to*
*Change Your Financial Situation*

Gerard Hoffman

# *Your Free Gift*

As a way of saying thank you for your purchase,

free Daily Habit Tracker for self-printing are available

to readers of this book.

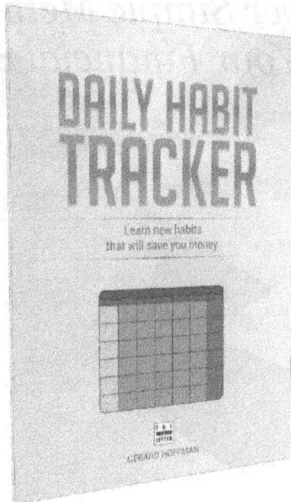

Enter the link below to your browser

to get free instant access.

https://mailchi.mp/b409dff6b06b/your-free-gift

# *Contents*

# *Introduction*

It's Saturday night, your friends are all going out, but you can't afford to join them. You have trouble falling asleep at night, your mind, racing about how you're going to pay the rent or buy groceries. You take the bus because you can't afford a car, and you worry about unexpected expenses or emergencies because you have no savings. Your financial situation makes you feel trapped and helpless. You work hard, but it doesn't seem to matter – you keep finding yourself falling further and further behind. You may even be a relatively high earner, but you *still* can't seem to save money.

Does any of this sound familiar?
Of course it does – that's why you picked up this book!

Before we go any further, congratulate yourself, because you have just taken the first step toward a brighter financial future. Don't criticize yourself for past mistakes; focus on the fact that you are now ready to take control of your finances!

This book will outline the key strategies you need, to understand and organize your finances, get out of debt, and begin saving money. Financial independence *can* be yours. Contrary to popular belief, you don't need to make a fortune to reach these goals, and the strategies that I will be teaching here, are easy to follow.

I understand the journey you're about to embark on, because I, myself, have been in your position. I'm no stranger to financial problems, problems that overwhelmed me with a tremendous amount of anxiety. I worked hard, and still, the situation got worse – I just wasn't able to pay my bills. Like many people, I turned to credit cards. It seemed to be the only way to stay on top of my expenses and ease the strain I was feeling. Unfortunately, this short-term solution made the overall problem much worse. Now, I was caught in the cycle of debt familiar to so many of you: when the time came to pay off my credit card bills, I didn't have the money.

Seeing this situation unfold, I took out a loan to help meet the shortfall, but it only served to accelerate my descent into the downward spiral in which I was now caught. When payments on *that* loan were due, I was no more able to pay them than any of my other bills. I realized that another loan was not the answer. Having looked carefully at my expenses and spending, it finally dawned on me, that the only way I was going to be able to get out of this nightmare of growing debt, was to completely change the way I thought about money. It became clear to me that I had no real concept of budgeting: I spent money on impulse and overpaid for the things I bought. I was working so hard for my money, little did I know that only when my money was put into savings (and bearing interest) would it begin to work for me.

It wasn't easy, but gradually I began to form smarter habits when it came to money management. Today, I can say I am free of debt and live a financial lifestyle that once seemed totally out of reach. These habits were having such a positive impact on my life, that even friends started turning to me for advice. They, too, wanted to learn how they could turn *their* situation around. I now teach many people how to regain their financial freedom, and I'm regularly rewarded by calls and letters of thanks for my life-changing advice. Now, I would like to share my experience and knowledge with you. I have included the very same tips and tricks that many people have already used to save money. If you follow my plan, I can show you the way out of financial hardship. By using the habits you will learn in this book, you will be able to start a new life, a life without debt. There is no short-term fix; with dedication and perseverance, you will be done with money problems for good!

Most schools don't teach anything about money management (I know mine certainly didn't!), so it's no wonder that you might never have learned how to handle your finances. If you don't apply the fundamentals, no matter how much money you make, you will still be broke. That's why the majority of lottery winners quickly go bankrupt, or professional athletes (a well-paid bunch, to be sure) retire with no money – they never learned good money-saving habits like the ones I will outline for you here.

I will teach you, not only how habits are formed, but how they can be changed. Each of the smart financial practices taught in the book will be explained in a simple, detailed manner, so you will be able to implement them even with limited knowledge about money-saving. Regardless of income level, people tend to make similar financial mistakes - I will help you identify and avoid those mistakes. This book will guide you on how to: budget, reduce your expenses, set realistic goals, and comparison shop to get the best prices. Reaching those small, attainable goals, can be a great source of pride, and as you continue to meet these, they'll serve as a great motivator to move on to bigger and better saving goals.

What will this plan not do? It won't try to force you to stop spending money on the things you enjoy; instead, it will help you get the most mileage out of your money. You will learn to really think about what you spend, to *plan* purchases and not just impulsively buy things that catch your eye in the moment. I suggest reasonable lifestyle changes, such as cooking budget meals instead of getting takeout. My system to becoming debt-free is not predicated on the idea that you will achieve financial stability through a sudden, massive influx of cash. It is about *money management* more than *money-making* (though there will be some tips on increasing your income).

You may think you simply don't make enough money to save any. You may be struggling to pay your bills, so saving seems utterly unrealistic for you. Each month, the situation seems to grow increasingly dire: interest penalties pile up, late fees, even overdraft charges only make a bad situation worse. It may *feel* hopeless. You may *feel* more credit card debt or a high-interest payday loan are your only options. However, this book will change all of that. While I focus on habits that apply to saving money, the ability to adopt positive habits is a great life skill in and of itself, that can benefit almost any facet of your life. If you follow the steps outlined here, it won't be long before you see your life improving and reap the benefits.

Take a second…

Take this moment to imagine your life without the pressure of financial obligations you aren't able to meet.

Now, imagine having money in savings for emergencies – what it will feel like to be able to buy the things you most want. Picture a financially secure retirement – it feels great, doesn't it?

Then let's get to work! Start learning good saving habits and building your future of financial freedom! Stop letting your money control *you* and start controlling your money.

# *Chapter 1:*
# *Saving Money: I Know -*
# *You've Heard it All Before*

I know, you've spent your entire life hearing the advice "save money!" It's not news to you, but you may not have considered how much it could change your life. Saving money is one of the most important financial habits you can adopt, yet it is becoming increasingly rare. Surveys show that 58% of Americans have less than $1,000 in savings. Since you are reading this book, you are very likely part of that group. It's not too late to change your financial outlook, but it is vital to begin as soon as you possibly can. It's not just the vague "rainy day" you have to prepare for; it's *life*.

You must prepare for emergencies, retirement, but also to live your dreams. Saving money can allow you to live the life you truly *want* to live. The more money you have saved, the more financially independent you can be (…and independence is really just a fancy way of saying you are in control of your life).

# *Saving Provides Financial Freedom*

"What's your number?" You have probably heard this before, in the movies, if not real life. It refers to the 'magic number', the amount of money you would need to have saved to take control of your life; to quit your dead-end job and do what you *actually* want to do. Very few people have the luxury of doing their dream job, waking up each morning, *excited* to go to work. Do you dream of starting your own business? Being your own boss? Maybe you have always wanted to write a screenplay or start a bakery. Whatever your dream, it probably looks quite different from your present life. The obstacle standing between your reality and your vision is *money*. It's no secret that it takes a substantial amount of savings to open a business or finance a dream ambition.

You might be thinking that quitting your job to live your dream is an unattainable goal. It isn't. With sound financial planning and good money-saving habits, you can get there, but there are other kinds of financial freedoms to consider. Saving money is a means, not an end. The end? The end is a better life, a life you enjoy, and one luxury you can afford with good saving habits is travel. Imagine being able to take a vacation without going into debt, a guilt-free trip you can afford because you planned and saved for it. Spending time with the people you love, doing the things you enjoy is a freedom few people have because few people practice well-founded money-saving habits.

Another essential part of being financially independent is having the ability to make significant purchases in the right way. Expensive purchases like cars, houses, or boats are much easier to make if you are correctly prepared before making the commitment. The more money you have for a down payment on these big-ticket items, the less you will have to finance, and the less you will ultimately flush away on interest. If you have a cushion of savings, making the monthly payments will be far easier to guarantee. Once you own items like a property or car, you will need to pay for repairs and upkeep to get the maximum return on your investment. Car maintenance isn't cheap, but it is less expensive than the alternative; neglect routine maintenance, and you could end up with surprisingly costly repairs. So, before buying a car (or any other pricey item for that matter), make sure you have the necessary money saved to keep your possessions in good condition. If you own a home, you will need savings for repairs to protect your investment. You may also want to remodel or make other upgrades, which, in turn, increase the value of your asset.

One fundamental freedom that very few people talk about is the ability to decide what size of family you want to have, not merely be restricted to the size you can afford. Whether to have children and how many is an extremely significant and personal decision that people make based on a wide variety of factors. Still, more and more people are deciding not to have children simply because they cannot afford to. Make no mistake; babies are incredibly expensive! Saving money now can mean having more options when making life's most significant decisions. Weddings, for instance, are another one of life's biggest – and most expensive – moments. Planning ahead and saving can mean the difference between the wedding of your dreams and a budget ceremony at the courthouse …and of course, if you have children, you will want to afford them the same options for their eventual weddings.

When you think of financial freedom, paying for education may not be the first thing that comes to mind, but freedom is about *opportunity* – education provides that. Maybe your dream job requires that you go back to school. If so, you will need to start planning and saving now. If you have children or plan to at some point, you have probably already considered the ballooning cost of education. College is extremely costly, but so are private schools from preschool through to high school. Every parent wants the best for their child, and education is an undoubtedly necessary foundation for success. Ideally, as soon as you have a child, you can start a college fund. Still, if you *already* have children, start saving as soon as possible. With regular investments in a fund earning interest, the money can grow until your child is ready for school. Imagine the satisfaction that comes with the freedom to send your child to college, knowing they won't need to face the realities of crushing student loan debt.

No matter your age, it is never too soon to save for retirement. Recently, a friend told me of his ingenious plan to pay for retirement by robbing banks on his mobility scooter. He was kidding, but if *your* plan looks anything like that, it's time to get serious about preparing to pay for your golden years! Retiring early is quite possibly the most common dream of working people today. It is *so* common that it has birthed the FIRE movement, which stands for: Financially Independent, Retire Early. Remember the "What's your number?" question? The FIRE movement is essentially about knowing your number and actively planning and saving to reach it. You can then retire early to pursue a passion, a dream career, or simply do nothing at all. It's all about having the freedom to *choose* what you want to do with your life, instead of being forced into making need-driven choices. If early retirement is not necessarily realistic (or desirable) for you, you will still need to prepare for the latter years of your life; substantial savings will allow you to retire without worrying about how to survive. For many, the goal is to have sufficient savings for retirement, so that when the time comes, life's luxuries can be enjoyed to the full: travel, visiting family, and passion projects you didn't have time for during your working career.

# *Money Helps in Emergencies and Reduces Stress*

Money is, not surprisingly, the number one cause of stress in America. It's no wonder: about 25% of Americans do not have even a single dollar saved. Not one single dollar! Unmanaged, these financial problems can lead to anxiety and even depression. You may have fallen victim to this scenario in the past: your money was tight, then something unexpected came up, say a parking ticket, and you had to put the charge on a credit card. Then, interest fees piled up, and things quickly snowballed out of control. The anxiety caused by this situation really cannot be understated. Having lived it myself, I understand, and I don't want you to continue living with that unnecessary worry. By saving money, you reduce stress, which not only improves your overall quality of life, it improves your health. Stress is a killer – literally. It can cause digestive problems, migraines, and insomnia. It can lead to high blood pressure, cholesterol, and heart disease, which can cause a heart attack or stroke. It causes elevated levels of cortisol, the so-called "stress hormone," which impairs learning and memory. Seeing a doctor or filling a prescription costs money, so if you have no savings, you may even avoid treatment, allowing illnesses to progress. It's also no secret that money is one of the leading causes of divorce; therefore, saving money can have a significant impact on your romantic relationships. Financial strain and debt cause stress, and stress causes conflict. All of these risks can be reduced simply by having ample money saved!

One meaningful way you can reduce your financial stress load is by planning for holidays and special events like birthdays and graduations. Christmas (or whichever holiday you celebrate) comes at the same time every year, yet people are often caught totally unprepared and end up relying on credit cards to celebrate. You may want to have a dedicated savings account purely for these holidays and events; it will make it easy to see at a glance how close you are to your goal. (I will talk more about the benefits of having multiple accounts in Chapter 4.) Of course, because birthdays, anniversaries, and other holidays happen every year, you are never really done saving for them. Instead, it's about putting away a set amount each month, so you are ready for these celebrations when they do come around. The holidays are known to be the most stressful time of the year for many people, and being financially prepared can reduce the burden substantially, allowing you to truly relax and enjoy these times with your loved ones.

However, saving money is not only about things you expect; you must also plan – and save – for the *unexpected*. That might sound like something of an oxymoron, but we've all found ourselves suddenly dealing with unforeseen expenses. We can never know precisely what they will be or when they will happen, but sure enough, they *will* happen. Much like death and taxes, they are a certainty. These events range from a flat tire to a sudden illness in the family. Smaller emergencies, like an unplanned doctor's visit or unexpected home repairs, happen frequently. Yet, almost 40% of Americans would be unable to cover even a $400 emergency without going into long-term debt, according to a recent survey commissioned by the Federal Reserve. Larger emergencies, like a death in the family or a job loss, are hopefully rare in your life, but it is a lucky person indeed who won't experience at least a few in his or her lifetime.

When life does throw you one of these major curveballs, the last thing you want is to have to worry about money on top of everything else. If you had a family member suddenly become ill, you would naturally want to focus all of your energy on helping that person, not worrying about whether you can afford to take time off work and travel to be by that loved one's side. No one likes to think about these unpleasant possibilities, but unfortunately, that doesn't stop them from occurring. What *is* in your control – working toward your peace of mind, that will come with having money set aside for these eventualities.

One adverse life event that nearly everyone will face at some point is a sudden job loss. Yet, almost 4 in 5 Americans say they are living paycheck to paycheck, without sufficient savings to absorb any income disruption. Economic recessions are a fact of life, and they can happen for many reasons. A year ago, the US endured the longest government shutdown in history, with almost a million federal workers either furloughed or required to work without knowing how long it would be until they received a paycheck. We are only a little more than a decade removed from the onset of the Great Recession, the economic effects of which, still linger. On a smaller scale, companies restructure, close, or otherwise downsize fairly often, so job security can be an illusion. Few things are more stressful than unemployment, but you can mitigate that stress by being financially prepared. It is imperative to have enough money saved to cover at least <u>three months</u> of living expenses.

No one plans to get injured or seriously ill, but it happens – and it is one of the leading causes of bankruptcy. Even if you have excellent health insurance with additional options to cover things like wages lost after an injury or illness, the out-of-pocket costs can still be staggering. This sort of financial hit can snowball in the worst way: people who are financially unprepared for an adverse health event are often then unable to meet their insurance premiums, their coverage lapses, and are left in the terrible position of being ill, broke, uninsured, and consequently unable to access treatment. If this were to happen to you, it could not only be traumatic for you but difficult for your entire family. Having adequate savings can prevent additional stress and heartache, at a time when you are already dealing with too much of both. In the worst-case scenario, your family could still be left paying off your bills after you have passed away, because, sadly, in many cases, debt does transfer in that way. Saving money is not just the responsible thing for your future; it can impact your family for generations.

Because I understand you might be starting from zero, it's natural to feel overwhelmed when thinking about these ultimate goals, like financing retirement. That is entirely understandable. The crucial thing to understand is that every dollar you save is a benefit to you, and now that you have started your journey, you will progress faster and faster toward your destination of financial independence.

# *Saving Money Helps You Focus on Multiplying Your Money*

Having now broken down many of the reasons you need to save money, let's talk about the real purpose of doing it – make your money work for you. Ideally, you want to become less and less reliant on your paycheck. When your money is in savings, you will start to earn *interest*. "Compound interest is the most powerful force in the universe. He who understands it, earns it; he who doesn't, pays it." You may have come across this quote, usually attributed to Albert Einstein. He didn't actually say it, but he should have, as it couldn't be more accurate! Compound interest is how you make your money work for you so that you are earning money even when you're not working. In the simplest terms, it means you are not just earning interest on the money you put in savings, and you are earning interest on that interest. Compound interest, as you might imagine, is somewhat onerous to calculate. Still, if you have money in a savings account, you get a monthly statement from the bank showing exactly how much interest income you earned on your savings. Of course, the amount you make will depend on two things:

1 - the amount you deposit into the account and
2 - the interest rate you are earning.

I will talk more in Chapter 5 about account types that might earn a better rate, but for now, just keep in mind that any time you are considering opening a savings account, the interest rate should be one of your first considerations.

Ideally, you will eventually have money in both savings and investments, so your money will give you a substantial rate of return. You might think that investments are only for the very wealthy, but there are more modest options such as penny stocks and index funds that you can research when the time comes. For now, keep in mind that saving money is about multiplying your money. *That* is the mindset that will help you build a solid financial foundation for your future.

Money has something of a nasty reputation, but it's worth bearing in mind that money is inherently value-neutral. It is as good (or bad) as the person whose hands it is in, so think about multiplying your money to be a force for good, in not just your life, but the lives of your friends and family, as well as your community. Your financial legacy might not be something you have considered before, but it is a way you can make a lasting impact even once you are gone. One way to leave such a legacy is by establishing a scholarship in your name or donating to any charitable cause that is important to you. These are important ways of having a positive effect on the world around you. You might be thinking that financial legacies are just for rich people, and you don't have the luxury of dreaming of one. It might have been out of your reach before, but if you apply my teachings to concentrate on reducing your debt, saving your money, and watching it grow, there is no reason you can't – or shouldn't – consider your finances as part of the bigger picture. As with everything, start small. Charitable donations don't have to be large to make a massive difference in people's lives. The more you multiply your money, the more you have for philanthropy as well as your own welfare.

# *Chapter 2:*
# *Okay, I Want to Learn Good Saving Habits ...But How?*

By now, you've seen how beneficial and rewarding saving money can be. You're reading this book, so I know you're committed to change, but you might be wondering ...is it possible for you to change your financial patterns? It is! No matter your age, old dogs CAN learn new tricks. Don't worry if you feel as though you don't make enough money to save any, either. It is unlikely that you genuinely use every penny you earn towards necessary living expenses. Good saving habits are about learning to live *within your means* by trimming the excess, so you *do* have a bit to put away each month.

# *How Habits Work*

No matter what kind of habit you want to learn, the process works fundamentally in the same way. The good news is, you already know how to learn a habit, you just might not have thought about it consciously. Think about when you first wake up in the morning. What is the first thing you do? Whether it's letting the dog out, putting the kettle on, or making the bed, you likely do the same thing every day, in much the same way, and all without really thinking about it. That's because it's a *habit*. When you first walk through your door after work, what do you do first? Place your car keys down, pick up your mail, or maybe kick off your shoes? We do these things out of habit, and these habits comprise our daily routine. One study found that 43% of our daily activities are done through habit, so learning how to save money can become one more of many you already practice!

Essentially, habits are ingrained behaviors, subconscious actions that are part of a pattern of behavior. They are formed by repeating a behavior until it becomes automatic. This process can take time, so don't get frustrated if you feel like saving money isn't second nature overnight. Just keep at it, and as you see the positive changes in your life, it will become more and more instinctive. The goal of being financially independent will motivate you to save money. That act of saving money will eventually become habitual so that even when you have met a particular saving goal, it reinforces the desire to continue to save. *Keystone habits* are those that influence other habits. Saving money is a keystone habit because once you start doing it, you will: see your money grow, become more thoughtful about spending, and decrease your overall patterns of impulsivity.

## The Three R's of Habit Formation

There are three basic components to habit formation: **reminder, routine, and reward.** The reminder is the cue, the trigger that prompts the behavior. For example, when your phone rings, you answer it. The ringing is the reminder to take the action of answering the phone. The routine is the actual behavior. In the example of the phone, answering the call is the *behavior* initiated by the reminder. The reward is the benefit you get from the action, such as talking to a friend or receiving important information during a business call. You associate the reminder (the phone ringing) with the reward (having a conversation) and answering the ringing phone becomes a habit, something you do without conscious thought.

The main habit we are trying to form here is saving money, so let's look at how to apply the three Rs. First, we have the reminder. Because motivation can come and go with your moods, you want to choose a consistent, *reliable* reminder to save money. One idea for a reminder would be getting your paycheck. Getting your paycheck will trigger the action, or routine, of depositing a set amount in your savings account. The reward will be an immediate feeling of well-being because generating savings translates to less stress. There will be many other long-term rewards as well, such as having the money to buy something you really want. Nevertheless, pride and satisfaction in making a sound, a forward-thinking financial decision is already a substantial reward.

It's important not to worry too much about your long-term goals when you're just starting. You don't want to get caught up in feelings of failure or being overwhelmed. Focus on each step as you take it and simply get into the habit of saving money. I know it can sound a bit hokey, but try making a chart with your paydays written in, and put a checkmark after each one as you put some of the money in savings. That way, you have a visual reminder that you are making progress. If that doesn't feel right for you, try asking a friend to help encourage you and celebrate with you. If you're really lucky, you can enlist a friend or partner to take this financial journey with you, and you can encourage and assist one another as you form these new money-saving habits. Keep in mind that this will all get easier as you go along.

## *Creating Good Habits and Eliminating the Bad*

| How to Create a Good Habit: | |
|---|---|
| 1. Reminder | Must be obvious, attractive and reliable |
| 2. Routine | Make it easy to perform |
| 3. Reward | You must get satisfaction from the habit |

| How to Eliminate a Bad Habit: | |
|---|---|
| 1. Inversion of Reminder | Make it invisible and unattractive |
| 2. Inversion of Routine | Must be difficult |
| 3. Inversion of Reward | Make it as unsatisfying as possible |

You are not just trying to form the good habit of saving money; you are also trying to break several bad habits, such as impulse buying, overusing credit cards, and spending everything you earn. While you follow the 3 R's to develop good financial habits, you must use the inverse (the opposite) to break the bad ones. To get a sense of the process, let's look at losing weight, something which many of us have attempted before.

To be successful in any weight loss program, you must develop good habits, such as eating healthily and exercising, whilst simultaneously breaking bad habits like overeating and being sedentary. You can see how these work together, just like saving money and not overspending; breaking a bad habit is just a matter of replacing the undesirable behaviour with a healthy one. If you want to lose weight, one step is to use the 3R's to form the habit of getting daily exercise. The reminder is that you wake up in the morning, and you see your running shoes sitting next to the bed. You don't have to count on will power to motivate you; you simply do it at the same time each day. The routine is that you go for a run. The reward is that exercise releases positive brain chemicals, known as endorphins, and you lose weight. To avoid sabotaging the positive effect of exercise, you must break the bad habit of overeating.

To break this bad habit, start with the inverse of the reminder, making it invisible. Like the old saying "out of sight, out of mind," make sure you don't have junk food sitting around the house where you might see it and be tempted to eat it. The inversion of routine is that you don't eat the junk food because it is unavailable to you and not worth going to the grocery store to buy. You might have the will power to overcome driving to a store and buying cookies, but not enough to avoid shoveling them in your mouth if they are right in front of you. The reward is that you don't feel guilty for breaking your diet, and you lose weight. Eating junk food is no longer satisfying because it makes you feel guilty and that you have failed. Know yourself, your strengths and weaknesses, and tailor any habit forming or habit-breaking program to your individual needs. It's easy to see how this can be done when you consider the 'reward aspect' of breaking a bad habit like overeating. Consider your motivation for losing weight – do you want to lose weight for your high school reunion? Tape the invitation to the refrigerator door. Is it to fit into a swimsuit for a vacation? Visualize being on the beach every time you need motivation.

Now that you understand the process of breaking a bad habit, let's talk about some specific ways you can break bad financial habits. Suppose you have a pattern of shopping every time you get paid. You want to make payday shopping sprees as unattractive and 'invisible' as possible. Getting a paycheck has become a trigger for your shopping, so try setting up a situation where you're *not* reminded of it, for example, having it directly deposited into your bank (that way you never see it). Avoid looking at department store advertisements that come in the mail – throw them right into the trash. Don't browse online retailers or clutter your email with promotional newsletters. A good idea may be to schedule something inexpensive and fun for payday. That way, the idea of binge retail therapy loses its appeal – you have something better to do! Make these shopping sprees as unappealing as possible by figuring out the total amount of money you spent shopping on paydays in the last year and identify something you could have purchased with that money, something you would really love to have. You can even print out a picture of that item and carry it in your wallet, that way you are creating an *inverse reward* for the bad habit of payday shopping trips. The longer you maintain these good practices, the more habitual they become. As Olympic medalist Jim Ryun once said, "Motivation is what gets you started. Habit is what keeps you going."

## *The 21/90 Rule*

Habits are a matter of training your brain, and as with any other skill, it takes time for this to become second nature. The important thing is to keep trying. If you stumble, don't give up, just remember that all progress is not lost and you will achieve your goals if you stick with it. A rule to remember when it comes to habit formation is the 21/90 Rule. The rule gets its name from the understanding that it takes 21 days to form a habit and 90 days to make that habit a lifestyle. These are steps you can absolutely master if you understand a few key things. To succeed in forming a habit, and then a lifestyle, you must have a proper plan. This book will help you form a plan, one that is reasonable for you to follow.

In order to have follow-through, remember your motivation. Why are you doing this? Boil it down to the one or two most significant priorities for you, and keep those things in mind always. Of course, you will have many reasons for undertaking this financial transformation, but it helps to boil it down to the most important, to hone your mental focus and clarity. Remember that the only person holding you accountable here is you, so be honest with yourself about the habits you are successful with and those which need more work. If you do these things and believe in yourself, you can form the habits necessary for financial success. Although you may have ultimate goals, this truly is more about the journey than the destination, as you are likely to make use of the habits you are about to learn throughout your life. Enjoy the journey, and that joy will make it much easier to make wiser financial decisions and live a freer lifestyle that you can maintain. Twenty-one days from now, you can have formed habits for financial success. In *90 days*, you can have a lifestyle full of good saving strategies.

# *Chapter 3:*
# *Time to Tame the Budget*

By now, you're familiar with the psychology behind forming good money-saving habits, but you are likely wondering where to start. It can feel so overwhelming, so first things first, let's put together a solid plan. The first step will be learning how to budget, so you know *exactly* where your money is going. Only then, can you start to make decisions as to how to direct less toward interest payments (and things you don't need), thereby saving more. Sticking to a budget, allows you to avoid spending money you *really* don't have.

# *How to Prepare a Budget*

To put it simply, preparing a budget is about deducting your *expenses* from your *income*. Anything that remains can be saved. Firstly, you will need to calculate your income accurately. If you work a standard job with typical hours, you probably have a good idea of exactly what your income is. However more and more Americans are cobbling together a living by working several jobs and having additional streams of income (often referred to as 'side hustles').

In 2018, 36% of American workers participated in the 'gig economy' (the term for freelance and contract jobs). Some people do multiple 'gigs' instead of a full-time job; others work a standard day job but supplement their income by taking on freelance jobs. If you're part of this workforce, you might receive cash payments, which can be easily overlooked when it comes to accounting. Whatever the source, you will need to be diligent about recording your income, including any tips you might receive. Get in the habit of recording the amounts in one location, such as a notebook or computer spreadsheet; that way, you have an organized account of the money you are bringing in. Now that you know your income, it's time to have a look at expenses.

The two basic types of expenses are as follows: regular and occasional. Regular expenses are the *easiest* to calculate because they are easy to foresee. Some occur on the same day each month, like car payments, rent or mortgage, utilities, and insurance premiums. Others are not on such a fixed schedule, but happen regularly all the same, like dry cleaning bills, car maintenance and grocery shopping. If you've been paying these expenses with a debit or credit card, you can look at your recent bank statements to see what your spending patterns have been. Most banks can provide you with online statements – a convenient way to stay updated with what you're spending.

Once you have gathered the information, organize your expenses into categories, these could include housing, utilities, transportation, and food. Having your spending broken down into categories allows you to see where your money is going at a glance. Don't forget to include some fun! You want a budget you can stick to, so make sure you include a category for entertainment or your favorite hobby. This way, you have a bit of guilt-free indulgence, built into your plan – because you are only spending what you *can* afford and not taking away from money that is meant for saving.

# *Occasional Expenses*

When figuring out your expenses, remember to budget for special events such as holidays, birthdays and Christmas. It's also worth considering things you don't buy often but need nonetheless, like clothing, for instance. These outgoings might be a little harder to calculate than fixed bills, but it is vital to figure out a reasonable estimate and budget accordingly. To start, think about your occasional expenses and make a list, just go month by month (think about things like birthdays and graduations). When you've worked out your outgoing costs for each month, add them up to get the total for the year. Divide this yearly total by twelve to calculate the average amount spent per month; this spreads all expenses evenly throughout the year, making it easier to budget. Always remember the importance of being realistic when calculating your expenses so that you can budget accordingly, particularly for events such as Christmas and anniversaries. If you aren't realistic in your estimates, you may end up overspending – you'll be left having to choose either to: spend savings that you had earmarked for something else or, worse still, putting it on a credit card and paying all that interest! A great tip is to look at bank statements or records from last year; these can give you a better idea of what you need to budget for these occasional expenses.

Once you have a record of your income and your expenses, both regular and occasional, you can assemble your monthly budget. Again, you can use a computer spreadsheet or a notebook – whichever system you feel most comfortable with. Here, you can now figure out the difference between your income and your expenses; this will be the amount you should aim to put into savings each month. Remember, paying off debt is another form of saving money. Depending on your financial situation, it might make sense to focus on paying off high-interest credit cards or loans first but make sure you also begin building a nest egg of savings as soon as you can.

## *Track Your Spending*

Now that you have an idea of your budget, the key is to *follow it*. Tracking your spending is a necessary habit to form. Each night, make a record of every purchase made that day, no matter how small. Remember expenses like tips, coffee, yes, even that package of cookies you bought from the vending machine at work! It all adds up, so it pays to be thorough. There are handy spending apps you can get for your phone that will track your spending and even categorize the expenses for you. Using such an app and recording your purchases as you make them, might prove to be the easiest way, but choose the method that feels right for you. Some apps allow you to link all your bank accounts, meaning if a debit or credit is made on any of your accounts, the app will reflect it on your ledger automatically. You can include credit cards, debit cards, and savings and investment accounts. However you decide to track your spending, the important thing is to do it, *and* to be completely honest; you're only accountable to yourself in this, so if you cheat, you're only cheating yourself. Never underestimate how positive an impact maintaining *momentum* can have on your financial journey, so do your absolute best to keep it going so you don't undermine your efforts.

Remember, if you record your spending as part of your daily routine for three weeks, it will become a habit. After three months, it will be a lifestyle.

It is a good idea to check for errors periodically by comparing your bank statements to your daily records. If like many people, you use a debit card for almost all your purchases, that statement will be an asset in making sure you are accurately tracking where your money is going. It will also help you check there are no incorrect charges to your bank account. Suppose you see a charge for something you did not buy, get in contact with your bank immediately. After you've gone over your bank statements with your personal spending record, check the record against your budget. If you have spent less than budgeted in a category, consider depositing that money into a savings account. If you spent more than budgeted for something, investigate *why* and either adjust your budget, or your spending. If, for example, you spent more than budgeted for utilities like water or power, you could be more conservative with that utility (by adjusting the thermostat or taking quicker showers). Or if you really can't cut down on any waste, adjust your budget to reflect the higher cost for the future.

A thorough and honest record of your spending will allow you to reflect on how you are spending money. Maybe you spent money on things you really didn't need. Question the necessity of each purchase carefully. Could you have done without it? Could you have gotten the same result for less, for instance, taking the bus instead of a taxi? When you are thinking about each purchase, consider it in the context of the goals you want out of saving money. We'll talk more about your priorities in the next chapter, but you probably already have some specific motivation for saving money – after all, something prompted you to read this book. Whatever your goals, consider that each dollar you spend is a dollar you could have saved toward that goal.

# *Watch Your Savings Grow*

Reforming your financial patterns to save money is work, but it is rewarding work. Make sure you take the time to appreciate the fruits of your labor. Look at how much money you've saved; think about what that means for your security and financial freedom. It might seem like you still have so much to do but remember to also think of what you have accomplished. If you have been concentrating on paying off loans, take comfort not only in what you've paid but also how much that will save you in interest charges in the future. If you've been focused on saving for something specific (such as a vacation) – you can now recognize how much closer you are to your goal. Don't' forget to celebrate each step forward, even when it seems you still have so far to go.

It's crucial to keep in mind that your budget, which is already improving your financial situation, is an ongoing project. Just as it will continue to help you make smart financial decisions, you must keep it updated and adjust as you go. As you start developing smart saving habits, it's natural to be eager and take an enthusiastic approach. This enthusiasm might lead to 'over-saving'.

*"Hold on, isn't the goal to save as much as possible?"* you might be wondering.

Yes, but the keyword there is *possible*. You can't leave yourself with less than you need to pay your living expenses. If you do find yourself taking money out of savings every month to cover your bills, first make sure you are not overspending. If you aren't, it could be that you're putting *too much* of your income into savings at the start of the month. Keep this possibility in mind so that you can avoid it.

While you're getting into the habit of tracking your daily spending, look over your budget at the same time each day. This way, what you're allowed to spend, is always firmly in your mind for each category. In addition to these daily check-ups, allot time each week to do a more thorough budget check. If you suddenly shuddered at the thought of spending your Saturdays working on your budget, don't worry; it doesn't take a lot of time. A few minutes each day and a review once a week will keep you on track. These weekly sessions will allow you to keep an account of how you are doing for each expense, as the month progresses. Let's say, you're ten days into your first month of budgeting and you've already spent 80% of your food budget, this lets you know you need to slow down and be much more vigilant about that area of spending. You may need to make adjustments to your budget. If you are over-saving, figure out which categories of your budget you underestimated and make changes. It's natural to underestimate expenses a bit at the beginning of your budgeting journey because no matter how diligent you were in listing your expenses, you rarely come across someone who hasn't missed something. If you need to add a new expense, figure out if that will mean saving less or if it is possible to shave a little off of another category. In Chapter 7, we will cover ways to reduce your food expenses, so hopefully, you will find some helpful tips for cutting your budget there. We will also go through other ways to reduce your spending later in the book. As you implement those methods, be sure to adjust your budget to invest more money in savings. Remember that your budget should be more of a savings plan than a spending plan because the key is to spend less and save more.

Every month, you will want to set aside time to go through your budget in detail. Again, this won't take a lot of time, maybe thirty minutes or so, it may take longer when you're just starting out, though you'll quickly improve with practice. Take this time to look at how you did in the previous month and think about ways you can reduce spending, or how budget categories need to be adjusted for the coming month. These monthly checks will allow you to see your progress and reveal problem areas. The more quickly you identify and fix these problems, the more money you can save. During these monthly sessions, make sure you are checking your bank statements carefully. Check for errors, but also review each expense against your budget. If you have budgeted a specific amount for rent, for example, make sure that is the amount your bank statement reflects you paid. It's also a good idea to go over your bills line by line to see which expenses could have been avoided so that you can make smarter financial choices in the future. Highlight any expenses that you can't justify as necessary; that way, it is clear to you how much money you are needlessly spending. Sometimes seeing things in black and white – or bright yellow, as the case may be – can clarify things in a totally new way. By familiarizing yourself with exactly where your money is going, you will be better able to predict your upcoming expenses. Some expenses, like utilities, likely vary from month to month, but as you become an expert on your budget, you will begin to be able to estimate very accurately what they will be.

## *Try the Anti-Budget*

Hopefully, I've broken down budgeting into simple and straightforward elements, but if you really don't want to track your expenses, you can try an *anti-budget*. While I really encourage you to try to create a traditional budget, if you find it's just too much hassle, don't worry: you can still save money. Despite its name, the anti-budget is another type of budget, but even easier to track than a traditional one. One of the least time-consuming ways to anti-budget is first to choose the amount of income you want to invest in savings. Once you've set your goal, you would deposit this amount into the bank as soon as you get your paycheck. You would then be able to easily see what was left to live on for the remainder of the month. As it's likely you've been living without a savings plan up until now; you *do* actually have experience with this method, the only exception being that you weren't previously putting any money into savings. You simply spent what you decided to spend while being mentally aware of the bills you had coming up. In this sense, you have been anti-budgeting all along, and now you're just adding the step of first saving money. If you choose to do it this way, you should still track spending in some manner at the end of each month. After all, you have to understand where your money is going before you can start to make meaningful changes that will increase the amount you manage to save each month.

Another way to save money with an anti-budget is to divide your spending into categories like you would with a traditional budget. You choose the number and type of categories you want, but I recommend sticking to three to five as ideal. For example, you might choose the categories of saving, spending and charitable donations. Another example is saving, housing, transportation, entertainment, and 'other'. After one month:

1. Calculate the amount spent on each of your chosen categories. You might see that you spent 80% of your money, saved 10%, and donated

10% to charity; or, that you saved 15%, spent 40% on housing, including your mortgage and insurance, 10% on entertainment, 15% on miscellaneous expenses, and 20% on transportation costs (i.e. car payment, insurance, and fuel).

2. Think about your financial priorities and desire to save money.

3. Look at where your money went, and compare it to where you want your money to go.

Maybe you want to increase your savings, and your transportation costs feel too high. Now you know where you need to reduce your expenses. Repeat this process every month, and you'll see it working to bring you closer to your saving goals.

Anti-budgeting is more about the big picture and less detail-oriented than following a budget – while you decide on the broad categories you want your money to go to, you don't really need to look at individual purchasing decisions within those categories. Take transportation, for example, let's say you decide you want to spend only 15% in this category and still have the power to choose how much of that will go toward a car payment, how much toward fuel etc., without working those individual costs into a restrictive budget.

An anti-budget will help you save money, but if you have been spending *more* than you make and accumulating credit card debt, you need a detailed budget to get things in line. One strategy you might consider is to start with a traditional budget initially until you consistently begin to change your spending habits and save more money. Once you've got the hang of this, *then* switch to an anti-budget. This gives you more freedom from some of the hassles of the traditional way. It's even possible to use both a budget and an anti-budget together. It may sound as though they would cancel each other out, but they actually work very well in tandem. Traditional budgeting will allow you to have a thorough understanding of your spending within each category, and an anti-budget provides a broader overview of your finances. The critical thing to remember is that no matter which method (or methods) you choose, it's about really being *aware* of where your money is going. If you stick to whatever plan you feel is right for you, you'll be on your way to saving money and improving your life.

# *Find Ways to Cut Spending*

The less you spend, the more you save. Now that you are tracking your spending, even just with an anti-budget, you can start to focus on the most achievable ways to reduce your spending so that you can put more into savings. Ideally, you want to put 10 to 15% of your income into savings. If you can do more, that's great, and by all means, do, but it's more likely that you're starting from scratch and are going to have to make some adjustments to reach this savings goal. It's okay to start slowly; the point is to *start*. In making these changes, you'll see your spending decrease, allowing you to save more and more over time. When you look over your spending each day, think about what you actually need and what you can do without. This *isn't* about depriving yourself; you should be able to find ways to make cuts (ones that won't bleed too badly). For example, check around for the best cell phone plan. You might be able to get the exact same service for a much lower rate.

Try to focus on one spending category to start with and try to minimize spending in that category as much as possible. If you first look at transportation costs, for example, you could try taking the bus once a week instead of paying for gas and parking. Carpooling can be another great option because it not only reduces fuel costs; it also decreases any depreciation in the value of your car. If you are paying for premium channels from your cable provider, do you watch them enough to justify the expense? If you have premium channels AND pay for multiple streaming services, think about how much television you actually watch. We will look at other ways to save money throughout the book; the point is that as you look at your spending, ask yourself whether it's really necessary. Look at where you are meeting your budget and where you need to cut back.

# *Chapter 4:*
# *Setting Your Goals*

Now that you've learned how to save money by budgeting, it's essential to think about *why* it's worth the time and effort. What are your goals for saving money? Are you worried about paying for retirement? Are you planning a wedding (and honeymoon)? You've probably thought a lot about some of your goals – spend some time considering *everything* you want to save money for (both in the short-term and in the long-term). It's really worth fleshing out your money-saving goals and considering how to prioritize them. This should be the fun part! Some of your money-saving progress will be down to controlling your spending, and it is tempting to focus on only what you are giving up. Instead, look to all the things you will *gain*. Maybe you want that new car, perhaps you dream of owning your own home. Your saving goals will also probably change with time, so you will want to revisit and revise them every once in a while. Whatever you're saving for, remember that goal, and it will make every cost-saving measure feel worthwhile.

# *Keep Your Goals Realistic*

As you set out on this money-saving journey, you will likely have some big dreams – but you also need to be *realistic* about what you can accomplish and how long it will take. The main obstacle you want to avoid is becoming discouraged and giving up. It's important to *continue* to save, so think about your income and what is realistic for you to accomplish in the coming weeks, months, and years. It can feel overwhelming so remind yourself it's okay to start slow. Try just saving 1% of your income the first month, then increasing the amount by 1% each month.

First, choose one small thing that you can do without. One of today's typical expenses is the morning coffee run, where it's not uncommon to be spending $5 on a drink. If you are one of those people, just think: that's $150 *a month* (about $1800 a year that you could be putting into savings). I'll bet you can think of things you could do with $1800 that mean more to you than coffee. Cigarettes are another great example because smoking has such a high health cost as well as financial cost. Maybe you regularly have takeout delivered, paying not only the high cost of restaurant food but also a steep delivery charge and tip on top! Whatever you choose to give up, just think about how short-lived the satisfaction that item brings you is – and you should have no trouble putting the money toward savings instead.

## *Set a Small Saving Goal*

When you first start out saving money, set yourself a small, short-term goal that's easy to achieve. It should be something that you *can't* afford to buy right now, but something fun that you would really *like to have*. A new cell phone? A short vacation? Maybe it's a gift you could give to a child or significant other. We all love that feeling of giving someone special the gift they've been wanting – their joy will be your joy. The purpose of this first goal is to provide a reward to *cement* your savings habits. It should be something you can save for in a matter of months. That way, it won't be long until you experience the payoff, and it will further motivate you to save even more.

If your first goal is a new phone, calculate what you will need to spend. If the cost is $500, and you want to buy it in four months, you'll need to save $125 per month to reach your goal within that timeframe. By being clear and specifying which steps you need to take to get what you want, you'll make it much easier to follow the plan successfully.

# *Set Your Larger Saving Goals*

In addition to the small goal you set, you should also think about goals that are both short- and long-term. Short-term goals should be things you can save for in one to three years' time. Some examples of short-term saving goals might be taking a vacation or establishing an emergency fund in case of job loss or another unexpected event. An emergency fund is a *very* important saving goal. This is your lifeline when you face the kinds of emergencies discussed in Chapter 1. It should be your goal to have at least another three months' worth of expenses saved (six to nine months' worth is even better).

Long-term goals are those that will take more than three years to reach. These are things like a college fund for your child or saving for retirement. The amount of time it will take you to reach each goal will determine the best *strategy* for savings. For example, with short-term goals, a standard savings or money market account will probably be your first choice.

A certificate of deposit might be a good choice for goals that take a year or more to reach but still fall in the short-term category. The longer the goal takes to reach, however, the more you will want to consider investment strategies with better interest rates but potentially more risk. For retirement, an IRA might be the right choice for you. I will discuss some of these options in detail later in this chapter. Keep in mind, the importance of calculating the approximate amount of time it will take you to save for any single goal so that you can choose the best, most appropriate tool for investing and growing your savings.

Whatever goal you choose, make sure it is as specific as possible. Consider: what you want to save for, how long you expect it to take and how much it will cost. If your goal is to save for a vacation, you need to be precise and take into account any other relevant details (such as seasonal fluctuations in price) to calculate what the vacation will cost and when you plan to take the trip. That way, you can figure out what you need to save each month and reach your goal on schedule.

## *Set Priorities for Your Goals*

Right now, you might be thinking *"...save for retirement? I don't even own a car!"*

That's okay! I understand that, in the beginning, developing good money-saving habits to the point where you can achieve these big goals, may *seem* unreachable. Be that as it may, it's important to remember that like with every destination, you will get there *one step at a time.*

You can prioritize your saving goals in the way that feels right for you. If saving to pay off your mortgage seems overwhelming, maybe focus on paying off debts like credit cards and student loans first. Paying off debt will save you money and get you closer and closer to the day when you can put more savings into the bank. Once you have paid off your debt, you can then focus on larger goals like saving to buy a car. When you have reached that goal, you can begin aggressively saving to buy (or pay off) a house. If you know you will need to buy a car within the next year, but your child is a baby, then it makes sense to prioritize saving for a car over saving for your child's college education.

On the other hand, if your car is in good condition, but your child is in high school, it makes sense to prioritize the college fund. How you prioritize your goals is up to you, but it is necessary to have a clear idea of what your priorities are because those priorities will determine *where* your money goes. When you prioritize your goals, start with just a couple that are the most pressing. You can have many goals, but avoid having too many priorities, lest you become overwhelmed.

# *Choose the Right Tools*

In order to follow your budget and save money, you will need to use the right banking tools. If you create different accounts for different savings goals, it not only makes it simple to determine how much you have saved toward each goal, you can pick the optimum *account type* for that saving goal. For each account, think about things like fees, interest rates, and minimum balances. For short-term goals, you probably will want to stick to accounts like basic savings accounts, money market accounts, or certificates of deposit. I mentioned these earlier, so let me now explain some of the details of each one. Please keep in mind this is only a basic overview, and you should make sure you discuss the specifics with your bank.

Regular savings accounts have low-interest rates, but they are insured and have no risk. They also don't usually have minimum balance requirements (as always, read the fine print and make sure you know precisely what fees your bank charges for each account type). When choosing a savings account, try to find one with an interest rate of at least 1 to 2%. If the interest rate is *below* the rate of inflation, you actually *lose* money in the long-term, so make sure to check that isn't the case with your accounts. There are now insured savings accounts that allow you to boost your interest rate, simply by doing things such as visiting websites for investment advice or inviting friends to open similar accounts (with an added bonus if those friends actually open accounts). It's always worth bearing in mind that there are many different options to explore. With a standard savings interest rate, you might think it's just as well to leave the money in your main account. However, this is a bad idea, because you want to make it as difficult as possible to use your money on impulse purchases.

Money market accounts, which you might use for short-term goals, sometimes have higher balance minimums (such as $1,000 to $2,500), *but* they may also offer better interest rates than standard savings accounts. They are also insured, so there is no risk, but the interest rate is not much better than with a standard savings account.

Make sure you don't confuse a money market account with a money market mutual fund, which is a type of fund offered by investment companies and banks. These mutual funds are not insured, so you can lose your money.

Additionally, some come with debit cards or the ability to write checks. It's probably best to avoid these as it simply makes it too easy to spend what you could be saving. Ideally, you'll rarely withdraw money from your savings accounts, so it doesn't need to be as easy as swiping a debit card. Also note that there are other fees associated with money market accounts, so again, scrutinize each account carefully before making a choice. Certificates of deposit (CDs) offer a higher interest rate than savings accounts. Still, money cannot be withdrawn from them for a predetermined time period, meaning they would only be right for savings goals where you know you won't need the money before the CD comes to term.

For long-term savings goals, you may want to consider an investment account such as a 529 plan or an IRA, or securities like index funds, stocks or mutual funds. Investments like these can be risky because they are not insured, so you can lose money. However, they also grow *with* the market, so for things you are planning far in advance, these sorts of accounts may provide the best return. Even though they offer better interest rates than standard savings accounts, it's important to keep some money in a savings account for emergencies. As it's usually quite difficult to take money out of long-term investments and steep penalties may apply.

Be sure to familiarize yourself with what your bank has to offer. Don't hesitate to ask questions about anything you are unsure about; ask if they provide a service where you can get individually tailored financial advice. If your bank offers this service, you should strongly consider taking advantage of it. Find out about accounts with higher interest rates that they may offer, or other types of accounts that might be right for your needs. Some banks offer checking accounts with debit cards that round each transaction up to the nearest dollar and deposit the change in your savings account. For example, if you make a purchase of $4.87, your bank charges your checking account $5.00 and puts the 13 cents directly into savings. That change can certainly add up over time, so ask if your bank offers such an account. You can also inquire about overdraft protection by linking a savings account with your checking account. While I am confident that you will be carefully managing your money, mistakes happen to everyone. If you should overdraw your checking account, costly fees will result. By linking your accounts, the bank will take money from your savings account before charging any overdraft fees. However, do NOT rely on this feature for making purchases you can't afford; it is only a backup option in case of oversight. Remember that you can choose different account types with various features for different needs. Whatever type or types you choose, make sure to automatically transfer money from your checking account to your savings account each time you get paid.

# *Chapter 5:*
# *Make the Bank*
# *Your Best Friend*

As you figure out *where* you want your money to go, the key is to make it as easy as possible for it to get there. Reducing the steps necessary to get your money into savings and decreasing temptations to take it out can mean the difference between success and failure, especially as you start out learning these good saving habits. It is vital to formulate a plan not just for which spending priorities you want your money to go toward, but also for getting the money into the appropriate account for that particular goal. It's also important to start to think carefully about credit cards, as they are a sure way into debt.

# *Automatic Transfer*

Now that you have a budget and know how much you want to save toward each of your spending priorities, set up an automatic transfer with your bank. By *automatically* having the money transferred to savings; your money will be put into your savings account without you even noticing and out of sight where you are less likely to spend it. As this occurs consistently and automatically every time you get paid, it will greatly increase the chances that saving money becomes a habit. You likely have your paycheck directly deposited into your checking account, or you deposit it there yourself. The key now is to make it as easy as possible to get part of that money into savings. If the money is automatically transferred to savings at the same time your paycheck is deposited, you will be unlikely to notice the deduction. Meaning your checking account will be left with the amount you have budgeted to live on. If you have only one savings account, then you will simply transfer the amount you have earmarked for savings to one account, but if you have different accounts for different savings goals, think about how much you want to direct to each account. For example, if one of your saving goals is to take a $2,000 vacation in two years, set up an automatic transfer so that, each month, $84 of your paycheck goes directly into your vacation account.

If you get paid twice a month or more, decide whether you want to put part of the money from each check toward each goal, or if you want to focus on different goals each payday. For example, if you get paid twice a month, maybe your first paycheck each month will be for your emergency savings and alternating paychecks will be for vacation savings. Keep in mind that if you get paid fortnightly, there will be a few months out of the year where you will receive three paychecks. It's crucial not to treat these as 'free money', as they're part of the income total that you used to calculate and figured into your budget. You can choose how much to transfer, when to do it, and to which account you want to transfer it. The important thing is that you set up an automatic transfer in line with your budget and saving goals.

Of course, if all of your accounts are with the same bank, this is incredibly easy, but if they are with different banks, it's still simple to do. Follow the procedure for each of your individual banks, but it's most likely this will first involve linking the accounts. Online or in person, you will select the form for *external transfers*. Provide the bank that will be *sending* the money with the account number and routing numbers for the bank that will be *receiving* the money. From there, the sending bank will confirm that you have access to the receiving account, either by making a small deposit of one or two cents and asking for confirmation of this amount or by asking you to log in online so your password can be confirmed. This confirmation process can take a couple of days, but you will only have to do it once. It might sound like a bit of unnecessary hassle, but the upside is that you can then have money transferred automatically out of checking (where it could easily be spent) to savings. While automatic transfers are usually free, some banks do charge for transfers to other institutions, so it's best to check with your bank and ensure you won't be hit with an unexpected charge.

## *Saving First*

The key with an automatic transfer is that by doing it right when you get paid, you put that money aside *before* you get around to paying bills. It's unlikely there will be anything left over if you wait until the end of the month to make the deposit. After all, that's why you haven't already managed to save money; you've gotten used to spending all of what you have. Now that you've formulated a budget and determined what you will spend and what you will save, there's no reason to wait; put the money in savings as soon as it's payday and it won't be sitting in your checking account, tempting you to spend it on things you can do without! Once your money is deposited into savings, try to forget about it as you get on with your daily routine. Naturally, you want to take the time to celebrate the growth of your savings, but remember not to consider them an option for everyday purchases. If you don't have something figured into your budget, don't buy it unless you absolutely *must*. Remember to stay focused on the long-term advantages of saving, not the instant – but short-lived – gratification of spending.

## *A Direct Debit*

Another way you can set up your banking to make it easier to stick to your budget is to set up direct debits to pay all your bills automatically. Not only is this less bother than paying bills by mail – you can be sure they will be paid on time. Mailing payments can lead to late fees, either because you forget to write and mail a check, or because the mail takes longer than anticipated. Late fees are a terrible blow to a careful budget and a totally unnecessary expense. Even *worse* than late fees, paying bills late can result in service interruptions with additional fees to reestablish service. Being late on insurance payments can result in your insurance being suspended or canceled outright. Driving without auto insurance is illegal in many places, and you never know when you might need to use your health insurance, so it's critical to keep on top of your bills. Of course, even the most organized people can forget from time to time, so having the money automatically withdrawn from your bank account allows you to take bill-paying off your mind.

Some companies, including a few major car insurance carriers, provide a discount for setting up automatic payments. Paying your bills on time will help to improve your credit rating, an essential financial tool for life. The better your credit rating, the better the interest rate you can expect when shopping for a loan. Even a small difference in interest rate can mean a big difference in savings when making a major purchase such as a house or car that takes years to pay off. There are numerous advantages to using direct debit to pay your bills. Still, there is one thing to be cautious of: once an automatic payment is scheduled, it may not be able to be canceled at the last minute – make sure you are sticking to your budget so you never need to do this.

## *A Smart Savings Account*

As you progress toward your saving goals, you will get more and more comfortable with the habit, then the lifestyle, of saving money. In the beginning, however, you might be tempted to stray from your budget. Set yourself up for success as much as possible in order to stick to your plan. Outlined in Chapter 4 are the broad strokes of different account types, but consult your bank to find out their individual offerings. As with anything, if you don't find what you're looking for at one bank, try another. Comparison shopping for the account type that best fits your needs is definitely the right idea. Make sure you *are* getting the lowest fees and best services for your account. You work hard for your money and are working hard to save it, so as little as possible should be disappearing into your bank's coffers! When choosing a savings account to deposit money into, make sure there are as many obstacles as possible between your savings and frivolous spending. Find one with *restrictions* on taking money out. Try to make it so you can't take money from savings at the ATM, at least not without a stiff fee to discourage you. If you open a savings account that offers a debit card, decline the option or destroy the card as soon as you receive it. Many savings accounts have a limit on the number of times you can withdraw money each month before a fee is charged. That might be a good thing for you as it disincentivizes regularly taking money from savings.

Ultimately, your saving goals *will* take months or years to reach, so there should be no need to be tapping into that money in the immediate future.

Remember that there are many options for the type of account you choose. Make sure you do your homework and check out all the services your bank has to offer – talk to your banker to find the accounts that best fit your needs. If you feel as though you need a strong deterrent to squandering your hard-earned savings, you might want to consider something like a certificate of deposit. The steep penalties associated with taking the money out before the CD matures should make it easier to stick to your saving goals. You know yourself best, so be honest and realistic about how much help you need to avoid cashing out your savings for unnecessary expenses. The key with your savings account is to make it easy to deposit money and difficult to take money out.

# *Reduce Your Reliance on Credit Cards*

If you are a person with a lot of credit card debt, one of the most important ways you must begin reforming your spending habits is to cut down on using these high-interest money traps. It can be so easy to get credit cards you really can't afford to pay back and using them is even easier. The worst part about them is that they are so often used for unnecessary, impulse purchases. If you can't afford to buy something, do without it while you figure out how to save until you can. Almost 40% of Americans have credit card debt, and the median amount owed by each person is $5,700. The average interest rate for new credit card offers is 19%

and over 15% for existing credit accounts. The number is even higher for people with only fair credit, and it climbs higher still if you fail to make payments on time. That means that 40% of people are paying well over 15% interest on nearly $6,000! Consider the size of the hole that blows through any budget. The interest is even higher on store cards, so I strongly urge you to consider cutting up your charge cards and not taking any new offers.

Depending on your individual financial situation, consider keeping <u>one</u> lower interest card for emergencies, but remember it is only for emergencies until you can save enough money to protect you from any rainy day that comes your way. If you are tempted to use a credit card to buy something, think about what it will *really* cost. For example, if you use a credit card to buy a new cellphone for $1,000, and your interest rate is 18%, you will be charged $15 in interest for the first month after your purchase. While compound interest is our friend with saving money, it is the enemy with debt; the second month, you will be paying interest on *not only* the price of the phone but the previous month's interest as well, so 18% of $1,015 so your balance will now be $1,030. It's easy to see that the cellphone you thought was $1000 will end up costing you way more as interest charges snowball into a mountain of debt.

One option with existing debt is consolidating your credit cards into one monthly payment with a consolidation loan. Several services offer this, and using one can immediately increase your credit score while lowering your interest charges. A lot of people faithfully make monthly payments on their credit cards, only to see the balance grow each month. Whether you consolidate your cards or not, try to pay *more* than the minimum required payment each month. For credit cards and loans, paying more than the minimum amount due can save a lot in interest charges over time, so that is a great way to save money.

When it comes time to apply for a loan you need, like a mortgage or car loan, your credit score will be a critical factor but so will your overall amount of debt. Your debt to income ratio means that the amount of debt you are already carrying will be one of the things a lender looks at when weighing up whether to approve you for a loan and what your interest rate might be for that loan. As you work toward your saving goals, one of the most important habits to get into is to pay off *high-interest* credit cards, then keep your balance low by only buying the things for which you have budgeted.

# *Chapter 6:*
# *Your Home - The Money Pit*

Whether you own a large house or rent a small apartment, a lot of your budget probably goes to paying for your home and keeping it livable. You not only have to pay rent or a mortgage, but you've also got your utilities to consider, then furniture – it's endless. If you plan and strategize carefully, you can reduce these expenses. Previously, you may not have thought about how to get the best value for your money, but every penny you save on household expenses is a penny that can earn interest in savings.

# *Review Your Billing Statements*

It's possible that up until now, you've gotten used to simply paying your bills as they come in. With all billing statements, make sure you do a thorough monthly review, go over the charges line by line, to make sure there are no unexpected fees. If there are, call the company and either get an explanation that satisfies you or dispute them. Another great practice is to look over your bills with an eagle eye to see where you can cut expenses. If you still have a landline telephone, is it essential or can you save a few dollars and use your cellphone? Be wary of introductory offers that have ended, leaving you with a much higher bill than you initially counted on. Cable companies often have special rates designed to lure in new customers, but after the introductory period (usually around six months), the bill will increase to a rate that may not feel worth it for the service provided; consider whether you can go without it.

It is worth taking the time to compare competitors' rates. Perhaps you can get the same service for a much lower rate from another company. Take the time to do your research, and it might pay off in substantial savings. When it comes to renters or homeowners insurance, make sure you have the best package to fit your needs. Don't pay more than you have to, but also make sure that you have the proper coverage for your possessions. You don't want to save a little in premiums only to spend *a lot* in the event of your things being stolen or damaged. Different companies have very different coverage packages and rates, so shop around to find the best deal for your needs.

## *Negotiate Your Bills*

If you do find that you're overpaying for a service but can get the same thing for less from another company – don't make the switch just yet! First off, call your *current* provider and see if they are willing to match their competitor's lower rate. Most companies know that attracting new customers is both challenging and expensive - and you can take advantage of this to get a better deal. Customer retention is worth a little bit of give, which often means they will negotiate on rate and offer you a significant discount. If they won't, simply take your business elsewhere, but you might be surprised by the incentives a company will offer to prevent losing your custom/business.

If you have a service outage, whether it be cable or telephone, call up the company and ask for an account credit for the length of time you were without the service you were paying for. In my experience, it depends somewhat on the cause and duration of the outage, but, more often than not, companies are willing to offer some credit, making it worth your while to ask. For any real cost break, you might have to speak to a supervisor, but don't be intimidated by that; the reality is they are usually more frightened of lost business than a rank-and-file employee. Any time you try to negotiate a bill or get account credit, make sure you have the records in front of you so that you are able to provide facts to substantiate your argument. The more informed you are, the greater the chance of success in saving money.

One thing that you have great odds of negotiating is debt, especially *medical debt*. If you owe dues to any company, or you have a large medical debt, the owner of that debt will often settle for a substantially reduced amount (settling on something is better than nothing). Medical debt is something that hospitals and other debt holders are willing to negotiate on quite a bit, as usually the amount due is more than the person can afford to pay. They know they can't get blood from a stone, so they will often readily settle for considerably less. It's always worth a try, and if you go through hospital bills and other forms of debt charge by charge, you might find quite a bit of room to bargain.

# *Saving on Utilities*

Once you've gotten your utilities down to the lowest rate you can find, believe it or not, there's still room to reduce the monthly cost. With your power bill, for example, think of all the appliances that can be unplugged at night or when you're not home, to reduce consumption. Water heaters only take about an hour to heat the water in the tank, so unplug yours if you know you'll be away from home for any extended period (even if just overnight). Water heaters can be major culprits of a sky-high power bill, so you might see noticeable savings from putting yours on a 'power diet'. Washing your clothes in cold water also saves the usage of your water heater. When you cook, use the pot that fits your burner; using a small pot on a large burner, just wastes energy by making your stovetop expend heat unnecessarily. Use your oven as little as possible – it's an appliance that takes a lot of energy to heat. Consider a small toaster oven or cooking on the stovetop instead. Any time you leave the house, make sure you have unplugged chargers, laptops, and lights that don't need to be on. If, for security reasons, you want to have a light on in your home at dark, *invest* in a timer. These are easy to find at most hardware stores, and they only cost a few dollars. That way, you can have the light turned on for when you come home after work without leaving it on all day.

To save money on your heating or cooling costs, try adjusting your thermostat by just a couple of degrees. It's free to put on a thicker pair of socks in the winter, but keeping your house a balmy temperature? That can easily cost you big! On cooler days, leave the windows and blinds open, which will allow fresh air through the house; no need to use fans. Leaving the blinds open will let the sunshine brighten rooms, so you don't have to turn on electrical lights. In the summer, why not try opening windows to let the cool air in at night and early morning (and closing them during hot days). This will allow you to decrease your reliance on air conditioning – not only good for your budget but also great for the environment! Besides, it's cheaper and environmentally beneficial to cut down on your water usage. Try taking shorter showers, running the dishwasher only when it's full, and landscaping with water-saving plants or gravel.

To keep things interesting, why not try making a game out of saving on utilities. The aim of the game is to make each bill lower than the one the month before. As you start to see how much these savings add up, they'll soon feel more natural and routine. Just as you're building good saving habits, start working on the habit of trimming any excess on your utility costs. It might be beneficial in the long run to buy more energy-efficient appliances. If you'd like to explore that idea, read some tips below for how to get the best value for your money. Importantly, if you make energy-saving improvements, you can get a tax credit, so make sure you don't miss out on *that* money-saving opportunity. Things like energy-saving windows and furnaces can pay for themselves not only in direct energy costs but also by reducing your tax bill.

# Garage Sales

There are so many ways to buy quality goods at a discount and little reason to pay full price in most circumstances. If you go to a thrift store in an affluent area, it's not surprising to find designer items with the tags still attached (items that someone paid a fortune for and never wore) now available for a fraction of the original price. It isn't even necessary to leave the house for these opportunities. Social media sites such as Facebook have garage sale sections where you can browse for barely used items for sale in your area. This is an especially good idea for people who have young children who quickly outgrow clothing before it can even show wear. When your children are too young to be fashion- or brand-conscious, don't bother paying full price at a department store. Moreover, as you buy things in new sizes, sell the stuff they have outgrown if you don't have a younger child to whom you can pass them on.

Go through your house and look at things you may have that you don't need or use. Maybe you made the mistake of funding a hobby that turned out not to be right for you, or that you simply don't have time to indulge. Maybe you bought exercise equipment with the best of intentions, only to let it gather dust and take up space. What may be useless to you might be exactly what someone else is looking for, so consider holding a garage sale or listing items on Facebook or Craigslist.

# Buy Quality, Not Quantity

As you think about ways to save money, your instinct may be to buy the cheapest option available. After all, that's another way to save money, right? Actually...that may be wrong. In some cases (e.g. electronics or kitchen accessories) it makes sense to spend more to get a *quality* item that can serve you for many years instead of saving a few dollars on an alternative that will quickly wear out. When considering a purchase, think about how long you'll expect to have the item for and how often you expect to use it. The more expensive the purchase price, the longer you want to go before replacing it, and if you expect to use it often, you will need a reliable product. Also, consider the pace of technology and how quickly the item might become obsolete. With cell phones, for example, there are always newer models with more options being released to the market. Of course, what doesn't make good financial sense is to upgrade at every opportunity – but consider that electronics do rapidly evolve and how this limits the lifespan of their utility.

When you are preparing to purchase home goods, do your research: read consumer reviews to find products with the best performance and durability. Also, check the warranty conditions for your purchase – be sure to undertake any steps necessary to activate it, if this is required. It takes a few minutes, but if the product breaks, you may be able to get it replaced or repaired at no charge. When purchasing items that you will have in your home for years, keep in mind that saving off the top with a lower purchase price may end up *costing* you money in the long run. You want to do everything possible to get your money's worth with quality on the things that matter.

## *Comparison Shopping*

Before any expensive purchase, make sure to do your homework so you can be sure you're getting the best buy. First, make sure you research the best brand. Once you have determined exactly what you want to buy, make sure you look at a variety of stores. Not only will you see a fluctuation in prices between stores, but you will also even notice a difference in prices at different store locations. Walmart and Target may have the same item at very different prices, but you might find that a Walmart in one area is cheaper than a Walmart in another area. Each store manager is usually responsible for the inventory at just that location, meaning that same manager may put an item on sale, only at his or her store. There are many variables to consider, so it's worth checking out prices at a handful of stores. If you find that one retailer stocks an item for a lower price but you prefer getting it elsewhere for whatever reason, check if your preferred store does *price matching*. A lot of times, they will match the lowest advertised price for a specific item.

Aside from variability between stores and store locations, it's also wise to consider sales and *seasonal demand*. Store sales accompany most holidays, so plan ahead to take advantage of them! Try to make purchases out of season to save money. Christmas decorations are incredibly cheap *after* Christmas, and most will still be just as good for next year. If you're looking for an item that is most commonly used in the summer, like pool toys, you will likely find great clearance sales at the end of the summer. Think ahead and buy what you need for the coming year. Do some research on seasonal advantages for major purchases. Perhaps you are planning to buy something likely to have a back-to-school price reduction. If you need to buy a car, keep in mind that most dealerships do sales on the previous year models just before the next year's inventory comes out. Car purchase prices can be impacted not only by the time of year but the day of the week. Mondays are typically the slowest days at car dealerships, so sales staff can be more motivated to offer the best deals to make a sale on those days. In addition, late in the year and late in the month is usually the best time to find a good deal on a car. Whatever you're buying, consider how hard you had to work just to afford that item. Isn't it worth spending a few hours researching to get the best price? The amount you will save will likely be more than you could earn in the same amount of time.

# *Chapter 7:*
# *Tasty and Cheap*

As you begin to focus more on budgeting, you might be amazed at how much of your money is spent on food. Food prices have risen steadily, outpacing wage growth. While grocery stores are expensive, prepared food from restaurants is even worse! To get the most out of your money, making your own meals is essential. Eating out or getting take-out not only is bad for your wallet, but it's also bad for your health. By cooking at home, you can control things like sodium and fat, which can be excessively high in restaurant food. Simply cooking at home isn't enough, though; it requires a *plan*. You will need to carefully plan so that you don't spend more than necessary at the grocery store. Depending on your schedule, it might not be practical to cook every day. That's okay, but do make sure you have food you can easily reheat so you don't succumb to temptation and get fast food on the way home from work. With careful planning, it's only necessary to prepare food when your schedule allows it.

# *Meal Planning*

Before you grocery shop, make sure you have planned a menu for the coming week. By planning ahead, you can buy only the ingredients you need for the things you plan to cook in the next week. I like to cook a fairly large amount of something that reheats well, that way I can have a quick meal after work without having to worry about cooking more than a couple of times a week. Your needs may be different, but whatever they are, by anticipating them you can make mealtime stress-free. I'll bet you too, have played the classic game of 'what should I have for dinner' (not the most fun after a long tiring day at work). You can avoid that headache by sticking to your weekly menu. Going to the grocery store without knowing what you plan to cook can lead to *over*buying, with money wasted on food that will end up spoiling. Buying food on impulse is an excellent way to blow a hole in your budget, and, as a side benefit, planning ahead may also lead to a decrease in junk food purchases (you'll focus more on items you need rather than just what looks good in the moment).

If you have children, their schools likely send out a weekly lunch menu. If so, your children are already used to a menu system and might enjoy seeing what they will be eating for dinner in the coming week. If you allow each child to choose what they would like for dinner one day a week, the menu can be a family effort that everyone works on together. This might even make your children more willing to help with meal preparation since they're invested in the result. Anything that encourages time together is a positive for busy parents.

## *Homemade Meal-Deal*

Make sure you aim to buy as little prepared food as possible – swap a lunch bought at with food you bring from home. When you go to work, plan and pack a lunch, a snack, a drink, and whatever you need to leave you with no reason to buy from food vendors or vending machines. I personally find it's more practical to make my lunch the night before because mornings tend to be rushed; find what works best for you. In fact, that's something I want you to keep in mind for all aspects of money-saving: I can give you ideas, but tailor them to *your* life as much as possible, making them easier to adapt to and simple to stick with.

Avoid restaurants as much as you can, but when you do want to go out, check for the more inexpensive places that still get positive reviews. You'll likely stumble on some local gems that have great food and really could use some support from the community (as a national chain doesn't prop them up). These places often have more character but aren't all necessarily low-priced, so make sure you do your research to find one that is. Check out if they do any weekly specials or online coupons. Some places offer free appetizers or other incentives if you sign up for their loyalty program, which usually involves being on their email list. When ordering, try to avoid appetizers and alcohol, as this is where the cost can significantly pile up. If you stick to an entrée and drink water, you will still get more than enough food and not end up with a staggering total. For special occasions where you want to go all out with appetizers and drinks, could you go during happy hour? You might save a significant amount of money. As with everything, doing a little research and *planning ahead* when dining out can result in big savings.

# Zero Food Waste

Wasting food is bad economically speaking, but it's also something we all want to do better to avoid, there are too many hungry people in the world, and taking food for granted is a luxury they can't afford. Americans waste an average of a pound of food per person per day! Honestly…you might as well be throwing money in the trash. Of course, it's also harmful for the environment: water is wasted to grow food, pesticides are overused, and to top it all off food ends up in landfill where it releases methane – a greenhouse gas, destroying the ozone layer. Strive to *eat* everything you buy. Even if you plan a careful menu, you might not be able to buy the exact quantity you need. When possible, buy food from the bulk bins so you can buy as much – or as little – as you need. This can work out to be especially economical with spices. If you can't buy only the amount you need and you're left with an odd assortment of items, try freezing anything you won't use *before* it spoils. Then try to put together what you can into sandwiches or salads. I regularly eat something I call a Refrigerator Omelet, which is eggs plus whatever else is in my refrigerator and needs to be used up. No two are the same, and they are always good. If omelets aren't for you, try to find what works for you so you can use up all the things left in the refrigerator. Keep close track of expiration dates, so you don't let any food go bad (either cook or freeze it before it does). Don't automatically throw away food just because it has reached its best before date, however; those dates are approximate, so check if the food is still good before tossing it.

# *Make a List Before Shopping*

One of the times you are most likely to overspend on your budget is at the grocery store. Once you've made your weekly menu, go through and carefully list precisely what you will need to buy and in what quantity. Then make sure you only buy *exactly* those things. *Never* grocery shop while hungry – everything will look too enticing to pass up. If you find that even after carefully listing what to buy, you still buy things that aren't on your list, try using the free grocery pick up offered by many stores. You select the items you want from the store's website and then pick them up from the front of the store (so there's no chance to wander the aisles of delicious temptation). While pick-up is often free, delivery services are an expensive luxury, so try to do without them.

Make sure you do as much food preparation as possible. Don't buy pre-cut vegetables or meat. If you *are* pressed for time, invest in a slicer to do the work for you. It will pay for itself in no time. Avoid buying prepackaged kits, like those for pot roast or stir fry; instead, save money by purchasing the items separately. For things like meat, the most economical way to buy is usually to purchase in bulk, then divide the meat into the portions you need and freeze them. I find that buying at stores like Sam's Club or Costco often gets you the best deal on meat and other items you need in large quantities. They do charge for membership, but they often have specials on these that provide incentives. I purchased a membership at such a time and received an immediate refund of $30 of the $40 membership cost, meaning I effectively paid $10 for a year of membership. Be on the lookout for deals like these, especially if you have a large family to feed. Stick to buying only what you *need* in bulk; don't be tempted to buy extras just because they're attractively packaged or priced.

## Save Money on Substitutes

Where possible, try to buy the generic equivalents of big brands or labels. With things that you really love (your favorite coffee or Belgian chocolate), it makes sense to buy your favorite brand. These are priority items for you, you appreciate them, and that's okay. But do you really care what brand of milk you drink or what type of laundry detergent you use? Try experimenting with store brands, and you'll likely find that with most, you can't tell the difference from premium brands. You will learn which store brand items are just as good, and which ones you do want to splurge on. If you have children, try the following trick with cereals, crackers, and cookies: keep the empty premium brand box, then put the store brand food into that package. Without the package as a cue, they likely won't even know they're eating a less expensive brand, and you will be surprised at how much money you save.

Make sure that when you're buying a product, you check on the shelf price tag for the price per ounce. This will allow you to get the most out of your money, without having to do any complicated math in your head. Usually, larger packages are the best price per ounce, but not always, and, of course, if you buy a big package of something and only end up eating a quarter of it, you'll end up wasting a lot of money. Buy only the *specific* amount you need.

## Needs versus Wants

You often hear people say things like "I need my latte every day." Understand that a latte is a *want*, not a need. Your needs are things like basic food and shelter; most everything else is a want. I don't want you to think that you have to cut out everything you want from your life. First of all, no one would stick to such a plan. More to the point, that is the opposite of why you are saving money! The goal of saving is to be able to buy the things you *really want* - to prioritize, so you have enough for those things! When you think about things like a daily latte, a regular chocolate fix, or even a weekly trip to the hairdresser, think about your saving priorities. Ask yourself if those expenses are worth the money, or if it would be better to put the money in savings. If you are saving for a vacation, for example, would you rather have a week in Bermuda (or wherever you want to go) or chocolate? If the answer is chocolate, that's fine, just be sure you are aware that you can't have everything, and being honest about your priorities is the best way to reach your saving goals in the shortest possible amount of time. Try to cut down on the things that provide only momentary satisfaction in favor of saving for something that will *truly* improve your life.

When you think about the things that are most important to you, if lattes don't make it onto the list, try replacing that daily expense by taking coffee from home or getting a reusable mug and having it filled at your favorite coffee shop. Not all businesses offer this service, so be sure to check – some may allow customers to self-serve. Of course, coffee may not be your vice. Whatever it is, try to find a less costly alternative, either something you prepare yourself instead of buying ready-made or something you can choose to get less often. The key is really to identify what is most important to you *and* making sure that your money goes toward the important things instead of things you can easily do without.

# *Chapter 8:*
# *Shopping Time*

Shopping can be stressful and incredibly expensive, so the more you plan, the more you can save. By figuring out a strategy that works for you, you can save a lot of money on groceries and other items. Now that you have a weekly menu and know exactly what you need from the store, it's time to get the best deal possible on those items. When produce is in season, it's usually cheaper to buy it fresh, but when it's not, frozen is generally the better buy. If you aren't sure when different fruits and vegetables are in season, it only takes a minute to check. As you become more experienced at planning and saving, your grocery bill should see a steady and significant reduction.

## **Shopping Bags**

More and more stores are charging for disposable shopping bags. It's a small expense, but it still adds up over time. More importantly, plastic bags, as we know, are terrible for the environment. Invest in durable, *reusable* bags that you take with you to the store; they are only a few dollars, and they will pay for themselves pretty quickly. Even if the stores at which you shop don't charge for disposable bags, this is still a worthwhile habit to form in order to reduce the environmental impact. Some stores have put a moratorium on customers bringing their own bags, so be sure to check with the stores you frequent to make sure it's permitted. It's also smart thinking to buy one or two lined bags that are meant to keep frozen items frozen, particularly if you live a long distance from the store or live in a hot climate.

## **Pay in Cash**

If you have difficulty sticking to your shopping list and don't want to use store pick-up, one sure-fire way to make sure you won't spend more than you intend is to make sure you don't have the option. If you leave your debit and credit cards at home and take only the cash you have *budgeted*, you won't spend more than you intend.

Most cell phones have a calculator app – an easy way to keep track of your purchases, so you don't go over your limit. Spending cash also has a psychological component that is missing from swiping a debit or credit card. When you physically hand over cash, you cannot avoid feeling that you are spending money you worked hard to earn. If you simply swipe a card, it can have an unreal feeling of 'Monopoly money', making it all the easier to make purchases you will regret. The idea is to put as many barriers to overspending in place as possible so that you stay within your budget and meet your saving goals.

## *Spare Change*

I once caught my spouse throwing pennies in the trash. Believe me…we had a talk about it. Though, I can understand the impulse: pennies are such a small amount of money, and they can be a nuisance if you don't have a place to put them. It's time to get a piggy bank! Even pennies *add up*. Find a large glass jar or other large container and place it somewhere that is convenient. I prefer a jar with a very narrow mouth, so it's relatively easy to put coins in but not so easy to take them out. That's the idea – leave the coins there to accumulate into real money. Every day, put your change in the jar. After a few months or so, deposit that money into your savings account. The coins will have to be rolled before a bank will accept them, but this is a great family activity you can do while watching television. If you simply cannot find the time or muster the will to roll the coins though, Coinstar machines are an alternative.

These machines, found in most Walmarts and many other retailers, allow you to pour in the loose change. You are then provided with a printed voucher that you can cash out at a register. Be warned, though: if you lose the voucher, it's as if you've lost cash, so don't hang onto one with the idea you will cash it out later – do it right away. Also, the machine charges a fee, usually 11.9%, though this may vary by location. You do have the option of choosing a No Fee eGift Card, which can be used at one of several stores and restaurants. The goal, of course, is to get as much money as possible into savings, so only choose the gift card *if* you can use it to pay for something you were already planning to buy. This allows you to put the amount you would have spent into your savings account. It's best to roll the coins and deposit them yourself, but as I've said many times, do what works for you. If using a Coinstar machine means most of the money will get to savings, that *is* a win, and I'll take it.

# *Pay with Coupons*

When you look at your monthly budget, you will see expenses over which you have little control, like rent or car payments. One area where you really can have significant control is with the items *you purchase*, such as groceries and personal care items. Coupons are everywhere, and if you find a system that works for you, you might realistically be able to cut your spending by 35%. Coupons still come out in the Sunday papers, but they are also online, so check the internet by running a search with the retailer's name and "coupon". Many retailers offer large coupons on social media, so that's certainly worth a browse. However you find them, make sure you only save coupons for items you were *already* planning to buy. Otherwise, you aren't saving money…you are spending more! For example, if an item that you would *not normally* buy is $4 and you have a coupon for 50 cents off, you don't save 50 cents, you waste $3.50 on an unnecessary item.

Try checking the weekly ad circulars for stores in your area and look for great deals on products you already need. While it can be beneficial to shop around, going to countless stores probably isn't. You'll be spending fuel to drive around, and your *time* has value too. If you usually shop at Save World, but Bargain Land has something on your list with a buy-one-get-one-free deal, it may be worth making a stop there. You must then think carefully about whether an additional detour to Land of Savings, just to save 25 cents on dish detergent, will be as worthwhile.

Another thing to be cautious about is that you will often see coupons for *premium* brands that look attractive when even with the coupon, the store brand is still cheaper. Be careful not to spend more to save a little. Try to combine coupons with sales for even greater discounts. If the store has already marked an item down on sale and you realize you can save additional money with a coupon – you are now thinking like a frugal shopper. Some stores also have double coupon day where, just as the name suggests, they will double the value of coupons. Check with your favorite store to see if they offer such an incentive.

Saving money is, in a way, your part-time job. Just as you earn money at your regular job, you are now learning how to make that money work for you. It takes time, but remember the phrase "a penny saved is a penny earned"? It's true. When you put it into perspective, the time you spend locating coupons is worth it – it all helps to augment the hard-earned savings that you've worked for. To get the most savings, try using a cash-back saving app like Ibotta or Checkout 51. These apps are free and very simple to use: simply scan your receipt, and the app gives you rebates on select items.

Another plus is they work for more than just groceries, but also shoes and even electronics. The app deposits your rebates to Paypal or Venmo, where you can then transfer it to savings. These apps are easy and free, so there's no drawback to using them, even if clipping coupons isn't really for you.

You are probably already familiar with pharmacy and grocery store loyalty cards...you guessed it – they are another excellent way to reduce your bill! They require that you sign up, usually just by providing your name and telephone number or email address. Once you do, the store will give you a card that you can keep in your wallet to be scanned at checkout. Usually, you need to have a rewards card to take advantage of sale prices, so they are worth signing up for. Kroger affiliates offer Free Download Fridays, where a rewards card allows you access to a different free product every Friday. A lot of stores have similar perks, so check with your favorite retailer to see what they offer. In addition to saving at the store, a lot of rewards cards come with fuel perks. Depending on what you spend at the store, you can save a little to a lot on fuel costs.

Some stores have apps you can download to receive additional discounts. For example, if you are an Amazon Prime member, you can save an extra 10% off yellow sale tag items at Whole Foods by scanning your Prime code in the Whole Foods app at checkout.

The important thing is to find what works for you, gain all the insider knowledge on which sales and coupons your store regularly offers, and begin to develop a system. At first, you might only see very modest savings, but if you stick with it, you'll see yourself saving more and more as you learn how to get the best prices on the things you buy.

# *Online Shopping*

When going to a traditional retailer, temptation lurks around every corner. I talked before about using grocery pick-up, but for other items, try buying online. Use a search engine to search for only the products you need, and *don't browse*! Stay focused on only the items you have planned to purchase – practice discipline and avoid getting sidetracked looking at other things. Furthermore, consider shipping costs as part of the purchase price and be careful you aren't overspending – some online 'etailers' offer free shipping on orders over a specific total. Don't buy things you don't need to reach that total; try making larger orders less often. Perhaps you have a friend or family member with whom you can *combine orders* to reach the limit for free shipping. Some companies, like Amazon, offer premium services like Prime that can reduce shipping costs, but this comes with a hefty price tag. Make sure you're getting your money's worth if you are signed up to this type of service.

Any time you make an online purchase, make sure your credit card information is not saved. If it is saved, you can make one-click purchases. That's a bad idea! Even the little time and effort it takes to get your wallet, find your debit or credit card, and enter the information may be enough to get you to pause and think twice about whether you really want the item.

Also, make sure your billing information isn't saved on your phone for the same reason – it simply makes it too easy to spend money without thinking about it first.

# *Wow, a Super Sale!*

As Henry David Thoreau once said, "the price of anything is the amount of life you exchange for it." Imagine you see a pair of shoes or a watch that you simply must have. First, consider the cost of that item not in dollars but *labor*. Remember: time is money and money is time. If you earn $20 per hour, what do you take home after taxes? If it's, say, $15 per hour, you'd have to work 20 hours to buy a $300 watch. In other words, that's essentially two and a half days' work! When you think about the watch in those terms, is it worth two and a half days of your working life? When we view things this way, this style of thinking becomes an invaluable habit we can apply to small and large purchases. Before you buy a car, think about the number of weeks - years, probably – you will have to work to buy the car. Thinking of it in those terms might make a used car with a lower purchase price a more attractive option. On the other hand, you might decide that it IS worth the hours you need to work to pay for the item, and that's your choice – just make sure you are considering the true cost.

# *Chapter 9:*
# *Leisure and Entertainment*

You can't overlook the importance of having a bit of fun – but it's even sweeter when you do while getting the most for your money. I don't want you to think you need to live a depressing life just to save, so this chapter is about how to find low-cost entertainment and how to cut down on things that don't really bring you joy – leaving you with more money for fun *and* savings. It's also important to recognize how companies exploit you with targeted emails, mailers, and ads – *opt out*, so you put yourself back in control of your spending.

# *Plan Your Day*

If you are going to spend a day out and about, make sure you have a plan and that you stick to that plan. By having a careful strategy, you can plan entertainment that's within budget. Don't give yourself time for things like wandering around shops, because you will only end up buying things you don't need. I have a glass bowl that has color-coded wooden sticks in it. These sticks each have an activity written on it, and they are coded for 'no money', 'a little money' or 'more money'. The 'no money' *green* sticks have ideas like walking on the beach or having a picnic in the park. The 'little money' *blue* sticks include ideas like going to a matinee movie, visiting the zoo during inexpensive times, or going camping. The 'more money' *red* sticks are more for special occasions when we want to splurge a bit, and they include things like going out for dinner. This way, when planning a day out, we figure out what we want to spend and draw a stick of the appropriate color for an idea. It's fun for us, but of course, you can use any method that works for you.

Learn what your area has to offer – do a bit of discovering! Most areas have a weekly newspaper supplement that lists the events happening in the coming week. Not only could you find inexpensive ideas for entertainment – you might broaden your horizons with new experiences and meet new people from your community.

## *Fun (but not) for Free*

When planning activities away from home, you don't have to take advantage of an offer just because it *says* it is free. Admission is free, but you might end up having to pay for an expensive meal or some other *hidden* cost, along with things like transportation and parking. Nothing is free, so be very careful to check for hidden fees. Time-share companies are notorious offenders with this: they offer you a free activity or meal, then subject you to a high-pressure sales pitch that will make the experience nightmarish, to say the least. Quite a few museums and zoos have genuinely free days where your entire family can enjoy the venue for no charge. Keep in mind, though, that parking and concession fees are still quite high, so make sure you plan for those. It might be especially tricky with children because, of course, they will want to buy high-priced snacks and souvenirs. Decide in advance what you are willing to do. For example, maybe you will bring your own snacks (check individual venue rules to make sure this is allowed) and your child can choose one souvenir under a certain cost. Time together as a family truly is priceless, and it's never too early to start teaching children about good saving habits. I promise you that when they look back on a day at the zoo, they will remember the penguins and tigers far more than the fact they couldn't buy sodas from the concession stands. If they understand the rules *in advance*, tantrums at the venue are less likely.

# *Memberships*

Review every service you have that charges you a fee. Perhaps you have a membership at a gym. If you don't use it often, consider cancelling it and saving the money. Many people join a gym as part of their New Year's Resolution, then never go! If that's you, cancel it. If you go to the gym often but only do one type of exercise, like running on a treadmill, look online for used treadmills for sale. The purchase price will quickly be worth it in the gym fees you save.

If you do use your gym membership often, then it's probably something you want to keep, but consider letting it lapse in the summer. In most areas, summer weather is mild enough that exercising outdoors is a viable and free alternative to expensive gyms. In the summer, there are all kinds of inexpensive recreational opportunities like having a day at the beach or flying a kite with your young children. Consider giving geocaching a try for fun and exercise.

Geocaching is a sort of digital treasure hunt where you use GPS to locate hidden 'treasures'. The treasures usually don't have any monetary value; it's just for fun! Look online for geocaching groups in your area.

Streaming services are another type of membership (like Netflix, Hulu, or Disney +). There are more and more streaming services being offered all the time, and the existing ones frequently raise their rates. It might have seemed worth it when you first signed up, but the price has drastically increased, and perhaps it no longer is. Try to minimize the number of streaming services you are paying for by choosing only your favorite and cancelling the rest. Also, consider cancelling your cable and just keeping one or two streaming services.

These and many other premium services offer free monthly trials to entice new customers, but the catch is that if you forget to cancel by the deadline, you *will* be billed. One way to avoid this while still take advantage of free trials is by using a *privacy service* like Privacy.com. These services allow you to share your real debit or credit card number only with them; then they assign a fake card number for each merchant, which will bill to your real debit or credit card. You can choose an option where once you use the fake number, it becomes invalid, or you can choose to have it automatically become invalid after one day, so if you use one to sign up for a free trial, that service will not be able to bill you when the time comes. That way, even if you forget to cancel, you'll avoid being caught off guard by the bill. You can also set spending limits per transaction, per month, or per year for each merchant! This is also a great way to keep merchants from having access to your credit or debit card, as several high-profile hacks of large merchants have recently demonstrated that information may not be safe in their hands. These privacy services make it very easy to turn off a subscription service with one click, so you don't have to deal with the hoops such subscription services often want to make you jump through to cancel service.

## The 'Unsubscribe' Button

As I've said before, know the limits of your self-control to reduce the temptation to overspend. If you are on any mailing lists that send you catalogs, ask that your name be removed from their mailing list. If you get emails from companies advertising sales, unsubscribe if they make you feel tempted. It is not the wisest financial decision to 'take advantage of a sale' if you don't need the item; in actuality, the sale is taking advantage of *you*. Don't browse on websites. Search for what you need and stay focused only on that. However, clicking on the 'unsubscribe' button on emails can backfire by inadvertently verifying that it is an active email address, confirming to the company doing the sending that a real person is receiving the emails. If you know for sure that the sender is trustworthy, it's safe to unsubscribe simply by clicking on the appropriate button, but if it *is* an unsolicited email, do not open it, mark it as spam. This will tell your email software that you are not interested in emails from that sender.

If you find yourself tempted by prescreened credit card offers you receive in the mail, opt out by visiting the Federal Trade Commission's website at www.optoutprescreen.com. You can opt out for five years or *life*. This website also shows you how to get on Do Not Call lists for telemarketers, and how to make sure you don't get unsolicited commercial emails. It not only helps you avoid temptations to blow your budget, but it will also cut back on annoying, draining calls and emails that disrupt your evenings. That's a win-win, right?

## *Put a Stop to Ads*

Everywhere you go on the web, you likely see ads trying to get you to buy something. The ad algorithms have gotten very sophisticated, to an almost creepy degree. For example, if you do an online search for pet toys, you will see ads for pet toys and related pet items everywhere on the web for weeks to come. These ads are a major industry, designed solely to get you to buy things you *aren't* looking for at that moment. Whether you are on social media or checking your email, you aren't trying to spend money right there and then, but the ads are trying to convince you to do so. The good news is that it isn't hard to block these insidious ads.

Not only is it pretty easy to do, once you do it, it's done, and you don't have to worry about it anymore. For most browsers on Android phones, such as Chrome, simply click on the menu on the top right side of the screen, and then click on 'settings'. Scroll through the settings to 'site settings', click on it, and scroll down until you see 'pop-ups'. Click and then tap the toggle to disable pop-ups. Below 'pop-ups', you will see a section called 'ads'. Click on it and on the toggle, so that ads considered intrusive can be disabled. Whichever web browser or technology device you are using, just search 'how to disable ads', and you can easily find a step by step guide to blocking them.

Disabling ads is especially important when you understand how they are used as tools of psychological manipulation. Companies like Facebook and Google collect data on users, then sell it to advertisers. Those advertisers use it to target you with, in a very sophisticated manner. Social media and search engines can assemble a reasonably detailed psychological profile of each user, from political opinions to personality traits. Armed with that information, advertisers can then target you with ads that will very likely be persuasive. For a more specific understanding of how this works, consider that social media and search engine activity will *almost certainly* reveal a person's favorite television shows. Once the advertisers know that, they can look at psychological traits correlated to fans of those shows.

Suppose you like shows that correlate to introversion. In that case, you will be targeted with tailored ads that will psychologically appeal to people who tend to be introverted, perhaps with tag lines like 'beauty isn't always about being in the spotlight'. If, however, you like television shows that correlate to extroversion, you will get ads with tag lines like 'own the spotlight and feel the moment'. The information gathering is extremely extensive, so the targeting tends to be quite effective. When you understand how much time *and money* advertisers have spent learning how to profile and target you, you can see why you might have been so susceptible to those ads: you were meant to be. Now that you understand how they work, you can break down why it's important to disable them. It's not just because they have such a high probability of success, but because you now recognize they are designed to exploit your weaknesses, and that should not be rewarded.

It's valuable to recognize that ads are an attempt to manipulate you, so don't let them. In this digital age, companies share massive amounts of data on your spending habits, and you would probably be shocked at how much they can determine by *what* you buy, *where* you spend, and *when* you shop. If you're anything like me, you might find that intrusive. Case in point, don't reward these tactics by purchasing things you don't need just because an ad flashed a discounted item in your face.

# *Chapter 10:*
# *Who Doesn't Like*
# *Extra Money?*

No one, that's who! Of course, you like having that little extra in life, so in this chapter, we're going to look at some of the ways you can boost your money-saving abilities to the next level. Importantly, you need to change the mindset that a windfall of unexpected money is equivalent to spending money; instead, apply what you've learned to increase your savings, which is the ultimate goal. We're also going to talk about ways you can be more self-sufficient in saving money; it might even help you develop a new source of income.

# *Save Your Bonuses*

If you get a raise, a bonus, or a tax refund, don't increase your spending; increase *your saving* instead. As that money probably doesn't form part of your budget, try to put it all in savings. If you get a pay raise, you should definitely be able to save the extra income because you are used to living on less. When it comes to bonuses if you get these regularly and they're figured into your budget as a result, even if you cannot put all of it into savings aim to save as much as possible. It's a good idea not to figure bonuses into your budget as income, no matter how regular they are because they are *not guaranteed.* Tax refunds are often used for expenses one usually can't afford, such as new tires. Though I understand that, and it is a worthwhile expense, as you tame your spending, you should be relying less on this kind of refund for such expenses. Rather, they should be figured into your budget and planned for. Once you reach that point, add any tax refund to your nest egg of savings. It's particularly wise not to count on tax refunds because as government administrations change, so do taxes, and this isn't a dependable or predictable source of income.

I have mentioned this before, but it bears repeating: if you have budgeted more for something than it ends up costing – put the amount you saved into your savings account! As you employ the tips covered in previous chapters, your utility and grocery bills, as well as other expenses, should decrease. That is fantastic, but make sure that you are *saving* the difference, not spending it. Always think about the priorities you have set and stick to them.

## *Learn New Things*

Are you paying someone else to do things you could easily do yourself? Think of the money you could save! Online videos are widely available to teach how to do just about anything these days, so if you don't know how to cut your child's hair – watch a video. Are you thinking of hiring someone to do an oil change on your car? This would be an excellent skill to *learn* because it needs to be done regularly, and the price for the service is on the increase. Of course, your time is worth money too, so you don't have to live a lifestyle of total self-sufficiency. Still, you can increase your skillset in a few money-saving areas. Also, consider the barter system. Maybe you're great at mowing lawns, and your neighbor is great at cutting hair. Excellent! Find out if you can work out a trade.

Consider relying on your skillset for gift giving as well. Whether you make excellent jelly or have a talent for woodworking, give *homemade gifts* to the people in your life. Not only is it less expensive than buying gifts, it's also more personal and more meaningful.

## *Time comes with Your Savings*

I feel I can't overstate that your time is worth money. Your time is valuable to you, so you want to be getting the most out of it. As you organize your day, do the most important things first. On workdays, that's probably simple since your schedule is predetermined. Yet, do you find that after work and on weekends, you just watch television? Consider learning a new skill instead. You can use this skill to help others and make a little extra money. Remember we talked before about 'side hustles'? Maybe you are already a skilled photographer or cake decorator. If so, consider advertising those skills to make a little extra money on weekends or evenings. If you don't have a marketable freelance skill, consider *learning* one. Learning a new language is beneficial for many reasons, personal fulfillment among them, but you might also be able to command a higher salary at the job you already have. Alternatively, you could tutor for extra money.

There is always a demand for people to teach English as a non-primary language in person or online.

Think about what skills you have or have always wanted to learn. Now think of those skills in terms of a little added earning potential. Do some research into the things that interest you to determine where the *demand* is at, and which are most remunerative. Marketing a skill outside of your regular job can be a great way to meet new people, as well as make money. Try to find something you enjoy, so any money earned is just a bonus. Whether you enjoy crocheting blankets or creating websites, you might be surprised at how much you can earn just for doing something you love. There are numerous websites dedicated to selling craft items and many others dedicated to freelance work.

Do you ever take online quizzes? If so, did you know you can get paid for doing just that? Paid online surveys help companies learn what consumers are looking for, so consider doing some through a site like Swagbucks or Survey Junkie. Another idea is to take an introductory web development course online, then charge for small jobs on freelance sites. If you love animals, try pet sitting. Sites like Rover are always looking for dog walkers and sitters, so if you already walk your own dog, consider adding a couple more to your route for a few extra dollars. Thirty-minute walks can earn you $10 to $30, so if you live in a large city, you could make decent money without having to go far from home. Any time you do anything for free, consider whether there might be a way to get *paid* for it. You might be surprised at how often there is, and you can turn your time into savings in the bank.

# *Read About Finance*

While I have tried to lay out simple steps that anyone can follow to foster their financial independence, this book is merely an introduction. As saving money becomes more habitual for you, you will want to grow your *knowledge*, finding more and more ways to save. You will also want to learn about investment options that make sense for your level of income. If you have a commute to work, try devoting that time to podcasts on finance. Of course, there are many excellent books out there to help to expand your knowledge. At some point, you may want to consult a professional financial planner, but that may not be necessary if you do enough independent research. After all, any time that you can avoid paying someone means more money saved.

While I don't endorse any specific podcasts, I want to give you some ideas for getting started. *So Money* is highly rated for financial beginners – you can learn in simple terms that make sense while you are just beginning your journey. This podcast has a casual tone and includes real-life stories from the host and her guests. If your main focus is getting out of debt, try *The Dave Ramsey Show*. Ramsey's approach is known as 'baby steps', and he breaks down how to get out of debt in manageable steps so you can eliminate it and make a start on saving for financial priorities like retirement. *The Fairer Cents* is a financial podcast targeted to women, and it talks about issues that women face such as the gender pay gap and how caring for children can hinder a woman's ability to earn and save money. If you want to start thinking about how to invest money, *Money for the Rest of Us* is an investment podcast for beginners. Once you gain experience, try *The Disciplined Investor*, which is for people who have already been investing money for some time. To learn more about boosting your income, try *Smart Passive Income*. Be mindful that there are many others, so experiment until you find one that you enjoy. Listening to financial podcasts on your way to and from work is a great way to *make* that downtime profitable. The important thing is to continue your financial education; think of this book as 'Money Saving 101'. It's a beginning, a *foundation* for you to build on as you get started. Always be on the lookout for new ways to learn and save!

# *Live Within Your Means*

You may hear the phrase "live within your means" and simply shudder at the thought because you associate it with having to give up all the things you enjoy. It doesn't *have to* mean that at all; it just means you need to make smart choices (spend less than you earn, not more). Many people spend more than they earn and make up the difference with credit cards. What needs to be recognized is that this is not a sustainable lifestyle. If you've found yourself doing this, you might have to make some difficult choices to get to a less stressful, more financially stable point in life. Do this by boosting your income when possible, and by decreasing spending. When faced with giving up something you enjoy to bring your spending under control, consider the big picture. I am very confident that you have the desire – and the need – to change. You have read this far, after all. You wouldn't have done that if you didn't really want things to turn around.

I understand that living within your means is not the same for everyone. It might be relatively simple, or it might be quite difficult, depending on your level of income and your responsibilities. Whatever your income, make sure you follow the steps I have outlined, so you spend as little as possible. If you truly cannot make it on your current income, you need to find ways to increase your earnings or make cuts in your lifestyle, whether that be living with a roommate or trading in your car for a less expensive model. Whatever your situation, *take action* to live within your means and when your income increases, save more rather than spending more.

Think about a day that you enjoyed. Maybe it was a day you spent with your spouse or friends. Whatever it was, when you think back, which memories stand out? What brings you joy? I feel very sure that the part of the day that is meaningful to you is the person or people that you shared it with, or, if you were alone, a feeling you got from an accomplishment, like pride. I would be very surprised if you have fond memories of this day because of a thing that you bought or anything else that cost money. It really is true that the most important things are things that don't cost money. Learn to focus on *those* over material items, and it will become much easier to live within your means. The more you practice, the more it will become habit, then routine.

As you start to live within a sensible budget, you will become more and more familiar with the areas where you are overspending. Your newfound awareness of these habits can then lead to a plan for eliminating them. Why are you overspending? What is causing you to live beyond your means? Once you have addressed these questions, getting your spending reduced to a level below your income should be relatively straightforward. Make gradual adjustments in each area; reductions you are comfortable with until you're in a position to save money. Once you start saving money, allow yourself to feel the joy and pride it brings, as well as the reduced level of stress. Let those feelings motivate you to continue your money-saving journey.

# Chapter 11:
# Friends versus Money

As you focus on living within your means and saving as much money as possible, it's important to consider how your social relationships might be an obstacle to these goals. You need to ensure that your friends respect your desire to spend less and save more, and you can take steps to check they aren't getting in the way of your progress. Always remember that real friends *support* your goals. If your friends happen to be in a much higher income range than you, make sure they understand that your lifestyle cannot match theirs and you simply can't afford to do all the things that they can.

# *Pay Your Own Way*

One easy way to waste a lot of money is by going out to clubs or bars. If you go out for drinks with friends, the bar tab can quickly get out of hand. Buy your own drinks and *only* your own drinks. Of course, there are times when it's reasonable to buy a drink for a friend, but those occasions should be few and far between. For your budget's sake, it is better to stay home – perhaps take turns hosting your group of friends in your own homes. Alcohol is more expensive in bars and restaurants than it is at a liquor store – even before taking gratuities into account. If going out is important to you, take steps to minimize your bar tab as much as possible. Perhaps you can meet during happy hour when drinks are cheaper or try a less expensive brand of alcohol. Price and quality are not always directly related to each other. Look online for budget brands that get good consumer ratings and give them a chance.

The important thing is not to spend money you don't actually have, just to impress others. It doesn't work; you can't buy friendship, you'll simply be left with a staggering bar tab and empty wallet for your troubles. Be frank with your friends about the changes you are making in your life, and if they are your friends, they *will* understand. If you don't feel close enough to these friends to share such details, they certainly aren't important enough to blow your budget buying drinks for.

When you *do* go out, set a limit on what you plan to spend (and don't go over that limit). Make sure you only take cash, so you stick to your budgeted amount. Don't allow others to buy drinks for you once you've reached your limit, because this could lead to feeling obligated to owe them the next time you go out. Vow to only buy three drinks, for example, and drink them slowly, so they last the whole night. You could also try drinking water or soft drinks between expensive alcoholic beverages. It's a smart plan for your health *and* your wallet. The 'sober curious' lifestyle is catching on, so no one should raise an eyebrow if you decide to forgo alcohol altogether. Again, it is good for your health, and it will save you money. An even better idea is to offer to be the designated driver. You provide an essential service while still spending social time with your friends, and your soft drinks will likely be free, or at least very inexpensive.

# *Learn to Say No*

Try to channel your inner two-year-old and learn to just say *no*. It can be tough to learn this habit because most of us are raised to be polite and accommodating. Remember: real friends will understand if you need to say no when asked to spend money you don't have. Learning to say no can be incredibly hard if you have young children. Of course, you want to give your children everything, but in learning to say no, you model good behavior for them. Children learn through the example set by their parents, so explain that you just don't have the money for the item they are requesting. Another option might be to explain in terms of the bigger picture, for example: "we're saving to go to Disneyland, so if you don't get that toy truck, we can get there even faster!". Once you *have* said no, stick to your guns, otherwise you're just teaching them to keep pushing and cajoling until they get what they want. That is not exactly a desirable trait in children (and can be downright hideous in adults) so teach them that you have the final word and when you say no, they must respect that. Make sure you don't buy things you can't afford using credit cards just to satisfy their whims. Remember that your children love you, even if they're mad you won't buy them a toy.

Learning to say no *isn't* easy, especially if you're trying to break a lifelong habit of trying to appease everyone. No disrespect to the men out there, but I feel women especially are trained from an early age to be agreeable and accommodating. As a result, women might find it even harder than men to learn to say no. This isn't to suggest that men don't face this struggle as well, I would dare say it will resonate with many men reading this. Remember that learning to say no not only builds self-respect; it can also *earn* you respect from others. Studies show that people with low self-esteem tend to rate others' needs as more important than their own. If this sounds like you, you need to start recognizing that your needs are your *primary* concern. As they say on airplanes: put your own oxygen mask on before helping others. This may just as well apply to life in general – you need to be able to take care of yourself before you can take care of anyone else.

If you're struggling with the ability to say no, try rehearsing the answer that you expect to give. It could be something like "I'm sorry, but I can't go out tonight". You don't need to explain yourself; just be to the point and don't apologize repeatedly. If the person continues to try to talk you into changing your mind, recognize that person is not being respectful of your wishes and say "I said no". Remember that you are turning down a specific request, not rejecting the person making it, so there is no need to feel guilty. Be honest with yourself about what you want and know that no one will give it to you; you have to get it *for yourself.* If you want to save money, you have to take the necessary steps to do so. If a friend is asking you to go shopping and you don't want to because you don't want to spend money, offer a compromise such as inviting them round for a movie. Give yourself permission not to feel guilty for saying no – you're doing the right thing for yourself and looking out for your interests. When it comes to children, hearing no from you helps them to develop self-control. They will also learn to respect your authority as you set clear, consistent boundaries. Remember that giving in – to children or friends – only shows them what it takes to get you to cave. Don't establish that pattern. Stick to your guns!

When you can't afford to go out with friends, simply say so. Sometimes you might suggest a less expensive alternative, but real friends will understand and respect that your financial priorities have changed. I don't want to mislead you; you will have people who don't understand and stop calling when they learn you aren't up for going out. That's okay; those people don't truly care about you, and you don't need to have them in your life. They will only inhibit your ability to save money. Try joining a social group that doesn't have a membership fee, such as a bird watching or bicycling group. You will meet new people, get exercise and fresh air. Maybe you would enjoy signing up for a cooking class where you can learn to make inexpensive and delicious food at home. Another type of life change that is good for both your finances and your health. Whatever you're interested in, try to find free or low-cost groups you can join. If you can't find one, start one! Advertise on social media and with fliers on local bulletin boards. Chances are, if you are interested in a group activity, other people will be too!

## *Avoid Knee-jerk Reactions*

Make sure you don't spend money to compete with other people or to make your friends envious. Social media is especially good at fueling this because everyone shows the most positive version of their life, which may have little basis in reality. If you look through the social media posts of your friends and family, you will likely come away with the idea that they have wonderful lives filled with happiness and beautiful things. It's human nature to want to keep up, but remember that those social media pages are an illusion; people don't share their financial struggles or the feelings of inadequacy that lead them to post an unrealistic view of their life that projects perfection.

Don't feel pressure to keep up with your friends, and don't try to impress your friends with material possessions. Jealousy is unpleasant; you should not want your friends to feel it. It's natural to desire a certain level of envy from one's social group but try to recognize that coveting of possessions is the most fleeting and shallow kind. Wouldn't you rather have a circle of loyal friends who envy the work you have done to save money, to live within your means, and to *take control* of your finances? I can promise you that your friends will envy your financial position when you have ample savings not only for emergencies but things like vacations and retirement. They will be envious of the peace you feel from these life-changing steps, while they could find themselves dealing with anxiety over making ends meet – even if they buy cool stuff you wish you had. When I reformed my finances and started saving money, my friends were envious enough that they asked me to teach them how to do it too. I promise you that you can get there and you will find it much more satisfying than merely having your friends be jealous of your new shoes or car.

The phrase you used to hear being bandied about was 'keeping up with the Joneses', but now it's more like 'Keeping up with the Kardashians'! Reality television shows present you with a peek into the glamorous lives of pseudo-celebrities. These shows have a very materialistic angle. They are mostly about the stars looking fabulous and doing fabulous things, buying expensive clothes, cars, and houses. It may foster feelings of inadequacy in the audience members, especially young women. It can be tempting for these viewers to spend money to get a piece of what their favorite reality stars have – but those reality show stars have *a lot* more money than the average person does. It's important to remember they are aberrations, not aspirations. It might be called reality television, but that is not *reality* for 99% of the population.

Moreover, these shows do nothing to foster personal growth; very rarely do they show the stars doing meaningful things that genuinely benefit the community. Suppose you find yourself wanting to emulate your favorite reality television star, YouTube influencer, or even friends on social media…try unplugging. You might be surprised to find how much peace you feel when you don't have those unrealistic life models bombarding you with glimpses of their expensive lifestyles.

## *Establish Healthy Relationships*

One of the hardest parts of making good financial choices might be re-evaluating relationships that stand in the way of your progress. If you have friends that spend a lot more money than *you* can afford to spend, talk to them, and make sure they understand you can't afford to live that lifestyle. If they don't, or pressure you to spend more than you can afford, think hard about these relationships. Are they worth sacrificing your financial priorities for? Do these friends *care* about you and your happiness? If they are pressuring you to do something you have a good reason not to want to do, the odds are the answer to those questions is no. Surround yourself with people who support you *and* your goals. If you can have a social group filled with people with sensible financial priorities, it will make it easier to make wise choices for yourself. If you have trouble finding those people in your life right now, consider starting a group of like-minded people or go online to find a supportive community. Healthy relationships are necessary for a healthy and happy life, and relationships that pressure you to make bad choices are <u>not</u> healthy relationships.

# *Chapter 12:*
# *Are You Ready*
# *to Change Your Mindset?*

In order to save money, you will have to change the way you think about spending. Identify some of the *emotional* mechanisms that lead to overspending. Do you shop because you are impulsive? Maybe you're depressed, and spending money gives you a temporary lift. The phrase 'retail therapy' is typically used lightly. Still, it reveals a very real truth behind overspending: spending money is often an outlet for negative emotions, a way to try to fill a *void* in one's life. In order to stop engaging in these behaviors, it's crucial to identify the reasons and triggers for overspending.

# *Impulse Spending*

Impulsive spending is very, very common – so there's a good chance you have been guilty of it at least a little…if not a lot. That's okay; don't feel guilty, just resolve to change. We'll formulate a workable plan so that you don't spend money on things you'll later regret. If you see something you want to buy, don't. Instead, leave it on the store shelf or on the web. If it's in a physical store, take a picture of the item with your phone including the price, brand and specifications. If it's something you've seen online, save the web page on your phone or computer. Consider the purchase for <u>thirty days</u>. Think about where you will put it, what you will use it for, how often you will use it, and other necessary considerations. Consider whether it's likely to go on sale soon, because of an upcoming holiday or model close-out.

You might find that, after leaving the store or closing your browser window, you don't think about the item again. If that's the case, great! Taking a breather before making the purchase saved you real money. If, after thirty days, you still want the item, then buy it, but there' a good chance that your desire will have waned, especially as you weigh practical considerations like where you will put it and the need it will fill. If you do decide to buy it, be sure to look around to find the best possible price. If you saw it in a store, maybe you can find it cheaper online. Keep an eye out for store coupons that offer things like 10% off a total purchase, as well as coupons specific to that item. Check the manufacturer's social media pages to see if *they* offer any incentives.

## *Emotional Shopping*

Many people try to shop away negative feelings. If you are feeling depressed, anxious, or unappreciated at work, do you head to the nearest shopping center? If so, you are definitely not alone. People tend to spend money when they are experiencing negative feelings, but also as a way to celebrate when they are happy. Have you ever felt exhausted by a long week at work, so you told yourself you *deserved* to splurge on the weekend? Maybe you've felt displeased with your appearance at some point, so you bought a new outfit to boost your self-image. This is *emotional spending*. Just as you should never grocery shop while hungry, *never* go shopping while you are feeling a strong emotion – positive or negative. Emotions disturb your mental balance and inhibit good decision-making.

You can stop emotional spending by identifying your specific triggers. Maybe your job is a trigger because you feel unappreciated and overworked. If so, try talking to your supervisors about your feelings. Be respectful and honest, and you might get a satisfactory resolution. If not, try looking for another job. If that's not an option, try talking to a counselor about your feelings. You might be surprised at how much a good counselor can shift your outlook. If, on the other hand, a positive accomplishment makes you feel you've earned the right to buy something for yourself (that you can't afford) remind yourself that what you really deserve is financial security. If getting together with friends is a trigger to spend money, employ the strategies discussed above and have a frank conversation with your friends, then schedule alternative activities that don't involve browsing in shops. This doesn't mean you can never go shopping with friends, however. You absolutely can, just make sure you only spend what you can *afford* to spend.

For some people, shopping for emotional reasons turns into compulsive shopping, an affliction known as oniomania. The earmarks of compulsive shopping include spending more than one can afford for things they will neither use nor need. Feelings of joy, even euphoria usually accompany these compulsive shopping trips; those feelings are quickly replaced by the long-lasting guilt and shame prompted by overspending. If shopping is genuinely a compulsion for you, and you aren't able to stop on your own, please consult a professional for help. Do NOT feel ashamed; seeking help for an emotional problem is no different than seeing a doctor for a cold or flu. Taking charge of your life by addressing any issues you may have, then taking steps to fix them, is a sign of true strength.

## *Money Will not Meet All Your Needs*

If you are spending money to fill a hole in your life, recognize that going down this path will never work. You must address the actual problems you are trying to *cover up* by spending. One reason people spend money is to combat feelings of low self-esteem; when usually, spending money you don't have will only increase the frequency or intensity of those feelings. Instead, join a support group or talk to a professional. If you feel alone or like your romantic relationship/marriage is leaving you unfulfilled, money *cannot* fill that void. You must work to correct the underlying problem. Volunteering can be a great way to feel fulfilled and boost your self-esteem – it can make you see you are truly needed and can make a real difference in someone's life. If you are spending money for attention (buying a new dress because you have a strong need to be told you look fabulous) recognize that you're doing that because you don't feel great on the inside. Confidence has to come from within, not from a new hairstyle or fancy dress.

Another reason people spend money is simply that they're bored, but money won't fill that need either. Spending money might alleviate boredom for a brief period, but that time would be better spent learning a new skill or meeting new people in a social group. If you are a person who has spent money to cover up negative feelings, ask yourself honestly if it has worked. If it worked, did the negative feeling leave permanently, or just while you were buying things? Leaving you with debt on top of the previous problems you were trying to run away from? If you have bought things you didn't need just because they were on sale, have multiple items of clothing in your closet you have never worn, or you hide your spending from those close to you — you are likely shopping to fill an emotional void. Remember this old Filipino proverb: "If you make a habit of buying things you do not need, you will soon be selling things you do".

If you're spending money because you're feeling unfulfilled, vow to stop immediately. If you aren't able to stop on your own, ask for help. I know that therapists cost money too, but in this case, it *is* a worthwhile expense. As you work to cut down on spending money for emotional reasons, you need to address the underlying feelings you have been trying to cover up through spending. This is another occasion on which you might need to consult a professional for help; even if you can't change the problem itself, you *can* change the way you emotionally respond to that problem.

In addition to consulting a mental health professional, you might also consider volunteering at a food bank or soup kitchen. Not only will you be providing a much-needed service, but you'll also be getting a valuable insight into the lives of people who have virtually nothing. That experience can deepen the feeling of gratitude for what you have and give you a clearer perspective on spending money frivolously in a society where there is such imbalance.

## *Think Positively About Money*

You might have a negative relationship with money. After all, your desire to better your finances, indicates you've struggled with doing so in the past. It would make sense if you have come to think of money as an endless source of stress because you feel you never have enough. You might also believe that learning to save money means giving up so many things that bring you joy. Recalibrate your thinking – list the things that *truly* give you joy. I would be surprised if any of the items on your list cost money. The things that bring true happiness are family, friends, pets, and most of all, the feeling of being self-sufficient. However, I won't pretend that it isn't fun to buy a latte every day or several new pairs of shoes every week. If you're honest with yourself, you will probably admit the fun is very short-lived, but the burden of having spent the money lasts quite a while. Perhaps you've felt guilty for spending money on things you couldn't afford or ashamed at your lack of impulse control.

Try to think of money in terms of security, and the happiness that security can buy. If you have enough money to pay for your home and food, you have a secure place in the world thanks to money and good saving habits. As you get better at saving money, you will find that you don't miss most of those frivolous expenditures. As for the ones that you do miss, you won't need to go without them completely once you have a handle on living within your means.

## *Enjoy the Process of Saving Money*

In this book, we have talked about some steps toward good saving habits that might sound scary and difficult. Maybe you have never lived on a budget before, and it sounds depressing and overwhelming to try. Believe in yourself! You CAN do this. Don't strive for perfection because we all know that's unrealistic. Instead, aim for doing just a little better today than you did yesterday. Tomorrow, you will try to do slightly better than you did today, and on and on. If you can only save $10 a week, don't feel guilty, feel proud of the fact that you have gone from nothing to being on track to saving $520 a year! As you learn to cut your expenses, you will be able to save more and more.

There will probably be some missteps along the way, but that's okay. Don't beat yourself up, just think about what led to the problem so you can avoid it in future and get back on track. Remember that if you make a mistake, you won't be starting over from zero; you have learned and practiced strategies that will enable you to succeed. Think of your brain as a muscle: the lessons you have been working on have created a sort of mental muscle memory. That muscle memory will kick back in and help you make the right decisions again. All is not lost; you are *still* building on the good habits you have begun learning. Give yourself permission not to dwell on any mistakes; learn a lesson on how to do better next time and move *forward*.

While learning to save money can be difficult and involves making sacrifices, that effort and sacrifice, is in pursuit of a better, less stressful life of financial independence. Celebrate each step in your journey as a positive step forward in your life, a step toward living the life you truly want. Think about the options you will have as your savings grow. By thinking about saving as a positive, it makes the small sacrifices along the way so much easier to handle.

# *Conclusion*

First of all, I want to congratulate you for reading this book through to the end. That demonstrates that you have a real desire and willingness to change, and a commitment to learning to save money. Making that commitment is half the battle, so you should feel proud. Now you have not only the desire to change but the *tools* to do so. You are ready to make it happen! I hope I have inspired you to begin making positive changes and begin saving money so you can say goodbye to those sleepless nights of worry. I have given you the information necessary to make changes in your spending habits and begin saving money so you can be free from the tremendous stress that comes with debt and financial uncertainty. It's been my aim to make you feel that you *can* do it, whether you make $20,000 or $150,000 a year, whether you have massive debt or just haven't been able to learn to save. I can say this because I was once starting from a fairly dire financial state, I can understand that, at times, you were probably worried that this book would only work for other people, people who make more money or who have less debt. I hope I have made you see that this book is for people in even the worst financial situations, and now that I have given you the tools, you can make real changes. Once you begin making these changes, you will see an immediate difference in your life – a change for the better.

I know that you have been living for way too long with the stress of having insufficient funds to pay your bills and the anxiety of being unprepared for emergencies. You have probably been worried about how you will ever even begin to think about saving for retirement or your child's college fund. Now, you know how to create a plan that will lead to a new future for yourself, one free of financial stress. To make changes, you will have to learn new habits, but now you have seen how easy that is to do. I explained the process of budgeting, which is probably the most significant early step in learning to save more money. You now know your saving goals, large and small, and you have *prioritized* those goals. I have provided you with an overview of the banking tools to help you reach those goals more effectively. I have taught you how to make banking as simple as possible, and how to avoid overpaying for necessities like food and clothing. You have learned how to save on utilities, both by negotiating your bills and by cutting down on excess usage. I have shown you the importance of eating food prepared at home to save even more money and ways to use coupons to save at the grocery store. By trimming the waste from your budget, you will be able to save more and more as time goes on.

Remember that saving money does not mean you have to stop doing the things you enjoy. By carefully budgeting, you can cut down on waste and still have money for the things that are important to you. You will have to prioritize, but that allows you to grow savings for the things that are truly important to you. Think of this financial journey as a way to get the things you most want by saving for them, that way you will be able to have the things you desire and value the most while still living a life free of financial stress. You will learn only to make purchases when you can afford them, and that will take the guilt out of shopping. I also hope you have seen the value in considering all angles, such as when buying an appliance (do your comparison shopping and check for eligible tax rebates for purchasing an energy-efficient option).

I hope I have convinced you not to berate yourself for past mistakes, or *even* those you will make in the future. As you start out on your financial journey, you will be a beginner at first, and it is natural for beginners to make mistakes. Don't get frustrated; just keep trying! Hockey great Wayne Gretzky famously said: "you miss 100% of the shots you don't take". He meant that you cannot succeed if you don't try, so don't be afraid to try to build money-saving habits; it is the only way you will succeed. Also, remember that even a few dollars saved each week is an improvement and a solid foundation for more substantial savings in the future. Start small if you have to, just *start* – today even! Confront obstacles standing in your way. If your friends continue to pressure you to spend money even after you have explained you are working to save, consider whether those are toxic relationships that you would benefit from ending. If you have feelings of depression or low self-worth that are leading you to try to fill the void with material goods, know that you need to confront those feelings head-on before you are able to reign in your impulse spending. 'Retail therapy' is not beneficial, so try other forms of therapy or self-help.

While everyone has heard the phrase "money can't buy happiness", it isn't the whole story. Not having enough money to meet your expenses can cause a lot of *un*happiness. I don't want you to struggle with debt and the stress it causes for even one more day. This book has given you the tools to change, so start right away! A better life awaits you. This book has taught you how to begin saving money, and now it's time to put those lessons into action. Have you ever noticed that people giving financial advice for a living were once massively in debt themselves? They learned to save money and even turned their knowledge into a new career. Those people used to be just where you are now, so there is no reason you can't someday be where they are.

# *Leave a Review*

As an independent author with a small marketing budget, reviews are my livelihood on this platform. If you enjoyed this book, I'd really appreciate it if you left your honest feedback. You can do this by clicking on the "Write a customer review" button. I love hearing from my readers and I personally read every single review.

## Customer Reviews

**There are not customer reviews yet.**

| | |
|---|---|
| 5 star | |
| 4 star | |
| 3 star | |
| 2 star | |
| 1 star | |

Share your thoughts with other customers

Write a customer review

# *Resources*

American Bankers Association. (2020). Seven Tips to Establish Good Saving Habits.
https://www.aba.com/advocacy/community-programs/consumer-resources/manage-your-money/7-tips-for-good-saving-habits

Bank of America. (2020, June 3). How to Save Money - 8 Simple Ways to Start Saving Money. Better Money Habits.
https://bettermoneyhabits.bankofamerica.com/en/saving-budgeting/ways-to-save-money

Bank of America. (n.d.). Overdraft Service FAQs: Limits, Fees, Settings & More.
https://www.bankofamerica.com/deposits/overdraft-services-faqs/

Becker, J. (2019, October 30). 9 Reasons Buying Stuff Will Never Make You Happy. Becoming Minimalist.
https://www.becomingminimalist.com/buying-stuff-wont-make-you-happy/

Bibby, D. (n.d.). The Anti-Budget: A Less Stressful Way to Manage Your Finances. Money Crashers. https://www.moneycrashers.com/the-anti-budget-less-stressful-way-to-manage-finances/

Buchenau, Z. (2018). The Importance Of Saving Money: 15 Reasons to Start Saving. Be the Budget. https://bethebudget.com/the-importance-of-saving-money/

Buchenau, Z. (2020, April 24). What's The Point Of A Savings Account? Be The Budget. https://bethebudget.com/whats-the-point-of-a-savings-account/

Burnette, M. (2020, June 25). 5 Best Money Market Accounts. NerdWallet. https://www.nerdwallet.com/best/banking/money-market-accounts

Burnette, M. (2019, March 26). How to Transfer Money From One Bank to Another. NerdWallet. https://www.nerdwallet.com/blog/banking/how-to-transfer-money-from-one-bank-to-another/

Callaham, J. (2019, December 2). Here's how to block ads on your Android smartphone. Android Authority. https://www.androidauthority.com/block-ads-on-android-869724/

Clear, J. (2018, November 13). The 3 R's of Habit Change: How To Start New Habits That Actually Stick. James Clear. https://jamesclear.com/three-steps-habit-change

Coinstar. (2020, July 2). Cash in coins at Coinstar. https://www.coinstar.com/

Collingwood, J. (2018, October 8). Learning to Say No. Psych Central. https://psychcentral.com/lib/learning-to-say-no/

Consumer Financial Protection Bureau. (2016, March 18). What is a money market account? https://www.consumerfinance.gov/ask-cfpb/what-is-a-money-market-account-en-915/

Dollars & Sense. (2018, February 26). 9 Good Money Habits You Can Form. Mental Floss. https://www.mentalfloss.com/article/532663/9-good-money-habits-you-can-form

Federal Trade Commission. (2020, February 20). Stopping Unsolicited Mail, Phone Calls, and Email. Consumer Information. https://www.consumer.ftc.gov/articles/0262-stopping-unsolicited-mail-phone-calls-and-email#:%7E:text=If%20you%20decide%20that%20you,visit%20www.optoutprescreen.com.

Financial Fitness. (2020, February 5). How to save money for short-, mid-, and long-term goals. Cashay. https://www.cashay.com/how-to-save-money-for-short-mid-long-term-goals-125324096.html#:%7E:text=Short%2Dterm%20goals%20would%20include,and%20your%20life%20situation%20alters.

Fisher, J. (2017, March 24). 5 Money-Saving Tips from a Coupon Clipper. Kitchn. https://www.thekitchn.com/5-money-saving-tips-from-a-coupon-clipper-242916

Fontinelle, A. (2019, May 13). 5 Ways to Control Emotional Spending. Investopedia. https://www.investopedia.com/articles/pf/08/emotional-spending.asp#:%7E:text=What%20Is%20Emotional%20Spending%3F,any%20number%20of%20other%20emotions.

Gutierrez, J. (2017, May 9). How to form new habits using proven science. The Monk Life. http://www.themonklife.net/how-to-form-new-habits/

Hill, C. (2018, December 17). This is the No. 1 reason Americans are so stressed out. MarketWatch. https://www.marketwatch.com/story/one-big-reason-americans-are-so-stressed-and-unhealthy-2018-10-11#:~:text=Money%20is%20the%20biggest%20source, and%20just%2018%25%20blaming%20work.

Himmelstein, David U., Warren, E., Thorne, D., & Woolhandler, S. (2005). Illness And Injury As Contributors To Bankruptcy. Health Affairs, 24(Suppl1), W5-63. https://doi.org/10.1377/hlthaff.w5.63

Huddleston, C. (2019, May 15). 58% of Americans Have Less Than $1,000 in Savings, Survey Finds. Yahoo Finance. https://finance.yahoo.com/news/58-americans-less-1-000-090000503.html

Jennie. (2020, February 12). Anti-Budget: The Budget For People Who Hate Budgets. The Housewife Modern. https://www.thehousewifemodern.com/blog/anti-budget/

Jennifer. (2019, December 20). 15 Simple Money Saving Tips You Don't Know. The Intentional Mom. https://www.theintentionalmom.com/simple-money-saving-tips/

Jespersen, C. (2018, September 27). How to Use Coupons Effectively. NerdWallet. https://www.nerdwallet.com/blog/shopping/how-to-use-coupons-save-money/

Jacobs, T. (2017, November 13). How We Give Online Advertisers the Tools to Manipulate Us. Pacific Standard. https://psmag.com/economics/how-we-give-online-advertisers-the-tools-to-manipulate-us

Konish, L. (2019, September 24). New accounts aim to help you beat inflation. But you have to work for your money. CNBC. https://www.cnbc.com/amp/2019/09/24/new-accounts-aim-to-stop-inflation-from-eroding-your-savings.html

Lake, R. (2020, June 2). The 8 Best Finance Podcasts of 2020. The Balance. https://www.thebalance.com/best-finance-podcasts-4582978

Majewski, M. (2020, March 18). 5 Habits to Help You Live Within Your Means. Simple. https://www.simple.com/blog/savings-habits-to-help-you-spend-within-your-means

Martin, E. (2019, January 10). The government shutdown spotlights a bigger issue: 78% of US workers live paycheck to paycheck. CNBC. https://www.cnbc.com/2019/01/09/shutdown-highlights-that-4-in-5-us-workers-live-paycheck-to-paycheck.html#:%7E:text=Nearly%2080%20percent%20of%20American,report%20by%20employment%20website%20CareerBuilder

McCann, A. (2020, April 6). What Is the Average Credit Card Interest Rate? WalletHub. https://wallethub.com/edu/cc/average-credit-card-interest-rate/50841/#:~:text=The%20average%20credit%20card%20interest%20rate%20is%2019.02%25%20for%20new,WalletHub's%20Credit%20Card%20Landscape%20Report.

McCue, T. J. (2018, August 31). 57 Million U.S. Workers Are Part Of The Gig Economy. Forbes. https://www.forbes.com/sites/tjmccue/2018/08/31/57-million-u-s-workers-are-part-of-the-gig-economy/#19169b637118

Milman, O. (2018, April 18). Americans waste 150,000 tons of food each day – equal to a pound per person. The Guardian. https://amp.theguardian.com/environment/2018/apr/18/americans-waste-food-fruit-vegetables-study

Motley Food Staff. (2016, October 24). How to Calculate Monthly Accrued Interest. The Motley Fool. https://www.fool.com/knowledge-center/how-to-calculate-monthly-accrued-interest.aspx

Neighmond, P. (2014, September 22). Best To Not Sweat The Small Stuff, Because It Could Kill You. NPR. https://www.npr.org/sections/health-shots/2014/09/22/349875448/best-to-not-sweat-the-small-stuff-because-it-could-kill-you

Ontario Securities Commission. (2017, June 16). Plan for occasional expenses. GetSmarterAboutMoney. https://www.getsmarteraboutmoney.ca/plan-manage/planning-basics/budgeting/plan-for-occasional-expenses/

Pant, P. (2019, October 22). How to Save More Money Without Any Hassle. The Balance. https://www.thebalance.com/getting-into-money-saving-habit-4125552

Pearl, M. (2020, June 29). When is the best time to buy a car? Bankrate. https://www.bankrate.com/loans/auto-loans/when-is-the-best-time-to-buy-a-car/#:%7E:text=The%20months%20of%20October%2C%20November,quarterly%20and%20monthly%20sales%20goals

Privacy.com. (n.d.). Privacy — Seamless & Secure Online Card Payments. Privacy. https://privacy.com/

Proctor, J. (2020, June 12). 16 Fun Hobbies That Can Make You Money in Your Free Time. DollarSprout. https://dollarsprout.com/hobbies-that-make-money/

Scott, S.J. (2020, April 16). 26 Better Money Habits for Saving, Budgeting, and Increasing Your Income. Develop Good Habits. https://www.developgoodhabits.com/better-money-habits/

Turbo Tax. (2019). Energy Tax Credit: Which Home Improvements Qualify? Turbo Tax Intuit. https://turbotax.intuit.com/tax-tips/home-ownership/energy-tax-credit-which-home-improvements-qualify/L5rZH56ex#:%7E:text=You%20can%20claim%20a%20tax,from%202006%20to%20its%20expiration

Walmart. (2019, June 22). Frequently Asked Questions. Walmart Corporate - US. https://corporate.walmart.com/frequently-asked-questions#:%7E:text=Pricing,-Does%20Walmart%20price&text=Why%20is%20there%20a%20price,to%20compete%20with%20local%20merchants

What is 21/90 rule and how to use it effectively. (2020, June 1). AMoreThanLittleMotivation. https://amorethanlittlemotivation.blogspot.com/2019/01/what-is-2190-rule-and-how-to-use-it.html

Wikipedia contributors. (2020b, June 8). Habit. Wikipedia. https://en.wikipedia.org/wiki/Habit

Wikipedia contributors. (2020, June 7). 2018–2019 United States federal government shutdown. Wikipedia. https://en.wikipedia.org/wiki/2018%E2%80%932019_United_States_federal_government_shutdown

Youn, S. (2019, May 24). 40% of Americans don't have $400 in the bank for emergency expenses: Federal Reserve. ABC News. https://abcnews.go.com/US/10-americans-struggle-cover-400-emergency-expense-federal/story?id=63253846#:%7E:text=Almost%2040%25%20of%20American%20adults,a%20Federal%20Reserve%20survey%20finds

Zeichick, A. (2014, September 4). 5 things you should know about email unsubscribe links before you click. Naked Security. https://nakedsecurity.sophos.com/2014/09/04/5-things-you-should-know-about-email-unsubscribe-links-before-clicking/

www.ingramcontent.com/pod-product-compliance
Lightning Source LLC
Chambersburg PA
CBHW071652210326
41597CB00017B/2185